THE ABBEYS AND PRIORIES OF ENGLAND

THE ABBEYS AND PRIORIES OF ENGLAND

TIM TATTON–BROWN
JOHN CROOK

NEW HOLLAND

First published in 2006 by New Holland Publishers (UK) Ltd
London • Cape Town • Sydney • Auckland

10 9 8 7 6 5 4 3 2 1

www.newhollandpublishers.com

Garfield House, 86–88 Edgware Road, London W2 2EA, United Kingdom

80 McKenzie Street, Cape Town 8001, South Africa

14 Aquatic Drive, Frenchs Forest, NSW 2086, Australia

218 Lake Road, Northcote, Auckland, New Zealand

ISBN 978 1 84537 116 6

Editorial Director: Jo Hemmings
Senior Editors: Kate Michell and Charlotte Judet
Editor: Sarah Larter
Assistant Editor: Kate Parker
Designer & Cover Design: Alan Marshall
Production: Marion Storz
Cartography: William Smuts

Reproduction by Pica Digital (Pte) Ltd, Singapore
Printed and bound in Singapore by Kyodo Printing Co.
(Singapore) Pte Ltd

COVER AND PRELIMINARY PAGES

FRONT COVER: Furness Abbey, Cumbria. Infirmary.

SPINE: Gloucester Abbey. Cloister.

BACK COVER: Roche Abbey, South Yorkshire. View east in church.

FRONT FLAP: Forde Abbey, Somerset. The Hall.

BACK FLAP: St Etheldreda's Priory, Ely. Exhumation of the patron saint.

PAGE 1: Christ Church Priory, Canterbury. Vaulted ceiling with
heraldry.

PAGE 2: St Mary's Priory, Worcester. Chapter house.

PAGE 3: St Frideswide's Priory, Oxford. Boss from chapter house vault.

RIGHT: Wenlock Priory, Shropshire. View north–east across cloister.

PAGE 6: St Cuthbert's Priory, Durham. View south through main gate.

PAGE 7: top: Castle Acre Priory, Norfolk. View west in church; middle:
Glastonbury Abbey, Somerset. Abbot's kitchen vault; bottom: St
Swithun's Priory, Winchester. Paradise gate.

AUTHOR'S ACKNOWLEDGEMENTS

I am most grateful to my children, Hugh, Miranda, Lucy and Robert
(and to Anna, Hugh's fiancée) for word-processing my manuscript, and
for helping in various other ways; also to all the staff at New Holland
for much help and editorial advice. Once again, the most important
contribution has been John Crook's excellent photographs.

AUTHOR'S DEDICATION

For Veronica, in Spirit if not in mind.

Contents

INTRODUCTION

CHRISTIAN MONASTICISM started in the Egyptian desert in the 4th century AD, with St Anthony as one of the main founders. By the early 6th century it had reached Italy, and under St Benedict a famous monastery was established at Monte Cassino in AD 529. Benedict had started as a solitary hermit, but soon he attracted followers and it is for them that he wrote his famous 'Rule'. This told the monks how they should live their lives, and it had a very substantial impact on monasticism in Western Europe from the 8th century onwards.

Some early monasticism came to England from Ireland and Scotland, but it was the arrival from Rome of St Augustine and his small band of Italian monks in AD 597, that had most influence, and by the 8th century monasticism was flourishing in England, and had already found its first historian, the Venerable Bede.

Unfortunately the Vikings destroyed almost all the Anglo–Saxon monastic sites in the 9th century, but a great revival and reform of the monastic system followed in the 10th century, under the charismatic figures of Saints Dunstan, Æthelwold, and Oswald. At this time many of the greatest and most influential monasteries in England were founded or revived at places such as Glastonbury, Winchester and Westminster. Many of these monasteries also had a bishop (or the archbishop of Canterbury) as their head, and this was the start of the uniquely English system of monastic cathedrals.

After the Norman Conquest (in the summer of 1070), the extremely influential (and by now elderly) Italian monk, Lanfranc, was persuaded by William the

BELOW: *Abbot's chamber, Muchelney, with probable early 16th-century picture frame over fireplace.*

Conqueror and the Pope to come to England as archbishop of Canterbury. He rebuilt the church in England, including rebuilding all the monasteries, and creating important new ones like Durham and Rochester. Many monks were brought in from France, and all monasteries acquired the 'standard' plan whereby the key buildings (chapter house, dormitory, refectory and cellarer's range) were placed around three sides of a square with lean-to roofs to connect up the buildings. The nave of the monastery church occupied the fourth side, and the principal door into this led into the monks' stalls, which were at the focus of the *Opus Dei* (the work of God), as laid down by the Rule of St Benedict.

English monasticism reached a high point in the late 11th and early 12th centuries, and large numbers of new monks were recruited. At the same time a series of new Orders came into being. The most famous of these, and the most influential, were the Cistercians, who first reached England in 1128, and were soon to build vast new abbeys, such as Rievaulx and Fountains, in wild and remote places. As well as monks, they also attracted lay brothers to carry out much of the hard manual work.

Alongside this, many of the great non-monastic churches, which were staffed by secular priests, re-organized themselves into new semi-monastic communities, following the Rule of St Augustine of Hippo. The strictest of these Regular Canons, as they were called, followed the teachings of St Norbert of Prémontré, at 'Premonstratensian' houses such as Shap or Bayham.

ABOVE: *Fountains Abbey. View west along the Romanesque south aisle of the nave, showing remains of transverse barrel vaults.*

The most extreme of all were the Carthusians, though their main influence was in the later middle ages.

Throughout the 13th century rebuilding and enlargement work continued at most of the monasteries, but the initial fervour was beginning to leave the abbeys. At this time 'comfortable' new buildings were erected including even a special refectory (called a misericord) where meat could sometimes be eaten. The abbot was also beginning to acquire his own private house, as his status increased greatly.

In terms of the buildings, a new high point was reached in the early 14th century as can be seen, for example, at the magnificent new eastern arm of Bolton Priory, or in the Lady chapel at Ely, but the Black Death and famines of the later 14th century changed much. At least half of all the monks died, and the Cistercian lay brother system disappeared.

The monasteries of the later middle ages were very different places, with many monks living well in their own chambers, and the monastic estates leased out. The abbot was now a great lord, and in the final flowering of the monastic system it was most commonly the abbot's large palatial residence that was rebuilt. Many of the churches and cloisters (now much more comfortable with glazing in them) were rebuilt, and given fine vaults and large windows. A new era was under way in the early 16th century, when Henry VIII, unexpectedly, destroyed the whole system between 1536 and 1540.

TIM TATTON-BROWN

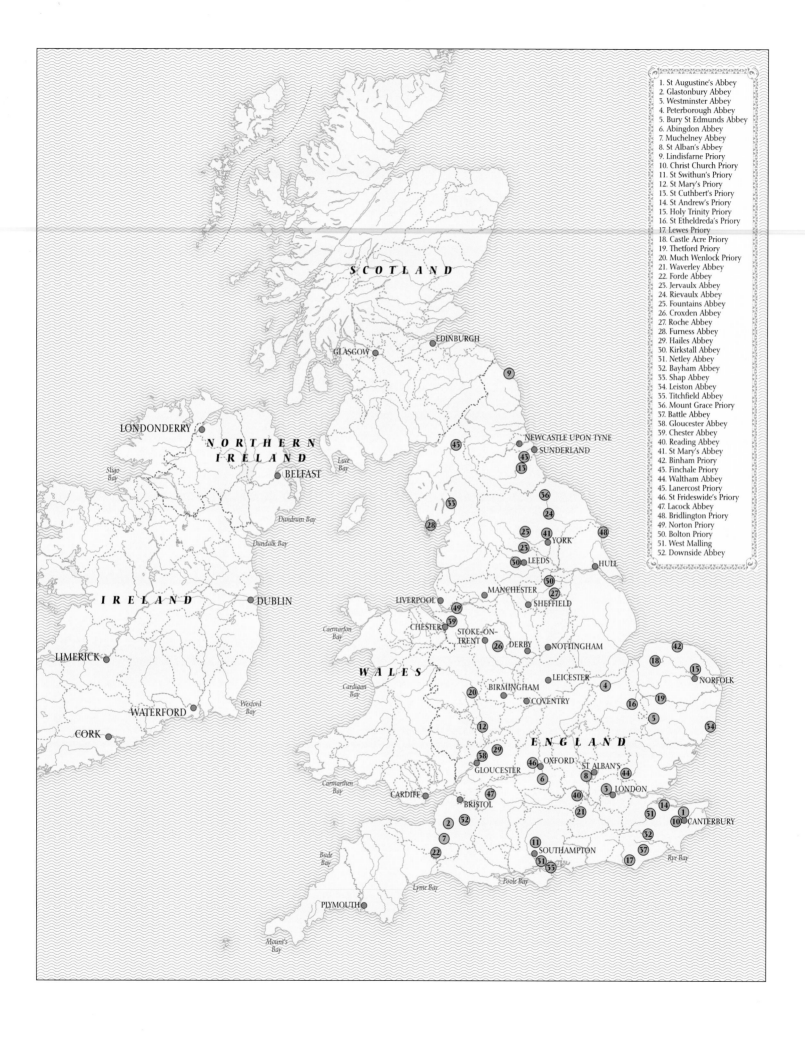

1. St Augustine's Abbey
2. Glastonbury Abbey
3. Westminster Abbey
4. Peterborough Abbey
5. Bury St Edmunds Abbey
6. Abingdon Abbey
7. Muchelney Abbey
8. St Alban's Abbey
9. Lindisfarne Priory
10. Christ Church Priory
11. St Swithun's Priory
12. St Mary's Priory
13. St Cuthbert's Priory
14. St Andrew's Priory
15. Holy Trinity Priory
16. St Etheldreda's Priory
17. Lewes Priory
18. Castle Acre Priory
19. Thetford Priory
20. Much Wenlock Priory
21. Waverley Abbey
22. Forde Abbey
23. Jervaulx Abbey
24. Rievaulx Abbey
25. Fountains Abbey
26. Croxden Abbey
27. Roche Abbey
28. Furness Abbey
29. Hailes Abbey
30. Kirkstall Abbey
31. Netley Abbey
32. Bayham Abbey
33. Shap Abbey
34. Leiston Abbey
35. Titchfield Abbey
36. Mount Grace Priory
37. Battle Abbey
38. Gloucester Abbey
39. Chester Abbey
40. Reading Abbey
41. St Mary's Abbey
42. Binham Priory
43. Finchale Priory
44. Waltham Abbey
45. Lanercost Priory
46. St Frideswide's Priory
47. Lacock Abbey
48. Bridlington Priory
49. Norton Priory
50. Bolton Priory
51. West Malling
52. Downside Abbey

ANGLO-SAXON ABBEYS
(Benedictines)

The earliest monasteries in England were built not long after the arrival of St Augustine in AD 597, though there may already have been a monastic site at St Albans before this. At Canterbury, uniquely, one can see the remains of the church built for St Augustine, as well as the empty tombs of his immediate successors as archbishop.

In the later Anglo–Saxon period, almost all the monasteries were destroyed by the Vikings, but in the later 10th century, five new Benedictine abbeys were built with royal patronage. This era of 'reform' was started by Abbot Dunstan at Glastonbury, but soon spread all over England under his zealous follower, Æthelwold, and other reforming Benedictine monks. By the end of the Anglo–Saxon period, most of the largest monasteries in England had been founded.

ABOVE: *A carved figure of the 1250s in the foliage scrolls that adorn the entrance into the Westminster Abbey chapter house.*

BELOW: *View south down the 13th-century passage between the refectory and dormitory of the cloister at Peterborough.*

St Augustine's Abbey

CANTERBURY, KENT

HISTORY

- AD 597 Founding of abbey by St Augustine
- AD 978 Church reconsecrated by Archbishop Dunstan
- 1070 Abbey refounded and rebuilt
- 13th century – Much rebuilding work done
- 1538 Dissolution of abbey and building of Henry VIII's palace.

SPECIAL FEATURES

- Remains of 7th-century church of St Mary and St Pancras.
- Early 7th-century archbishops' tombs
- Wulfric's octagon and early Norman crypt
- Later medieval gateways
- Fine on-site museum

ABOVE: *Detail of a doorway in the cloister west walk, which led to the abbot's lodging.*

RIGHT: *The lower walls of the octagon built by Wulfric II in c.1050. They were preserved below the floor of the Norman monks' choir.*

This famous abbey, the oldest in England and the earliest monastery in the country to follow the Rule of St Benedict, was founded by St Augustine soon after his arrival in AD 597. It stood immediately outside the Roman city walls of Canterbury, and became the home and church for the small group of monks sent out from Rome under Augustine's leadership by Pope Gregory the Great. Many of these monks subsequently went on from here to take Christianity elsewhere in southern England, among them the first bishops of Rochester and London. The church, dedicated to Sts Peter and Paul, was consecrated by St Augustine's successor, Lawrence, in AD 613; a few years later a second church, dedicated to St Mary, was built to the east, and beyond this another, dedicated to St Pancras. Amazingly, fragments, all of these early 7th-century churches can still be seen, including the north *porticus* (aisle) of the first church with the empty tombs of Augustine's immediate successors as archbishop, Saints Lawrence, Mellitus and Justus. These tombs

(now covered by a modern roof) were opened in September 1091, and the remains taken to new shrines in the Norman abbey.

The Anglo-Saxon monastery here became a great centre of learning in England, particularly in the late 7th and 8th centuries under distinguished international scholars like Archbishop Theodore and Abbot Hadrian, and this was perhaps the only abbey in England to survive the destructive Viking period. In the late Anglo-Saxon period a new octagonal rotunda was built by Abbot Wulfric II (1047–59), and remarkably the lowest walls of this building can also still be seen.

After the Norman Conquest a new abbot, Scolland (1070–87), was brought in from the abbey of Mont-St-Michel in Normandy. He demolished Wulfric's octagon and the church of St Mary, and built the eastern arm of an extensive new Norman abbey church on a crypt (which also survives). The large apsidal eastern end of this church was built to contain the shrines of St Augustine and the other early saints, and they were all duly translated here in 1091. Many new Norman monks were brought in at this time, and considerable expansion took place under Abbot Hugh of Fleury (1099–1124), who built a very large nave, with twin western towers, and also rebuilt the monks' main accommodation around the great cloister – the vestry, chapter house, dormitory, refectory, etc: the lower walls of all these buildings are still visible. The monastery was enlarged further in the late 13th century, as can now best be seen at the refectory, with the large new hexagonal kitchen built on its north side. At the same time, a grand new abbot's lodging was built for Abbot Fyndon (1283–1309) in the west range, and fragments of this can also be seen today, including the opening for the east window in the first-floor chapel. Just beyond the north-west corner of the cloister lies the abbot's great hall:

ABOVE: *Headless statue, from the on-site museum, of an archbishop (wearing his distinctive pallium), possibly St Augusine.*

RIGHT: *View north across the ruined nave, the Norman north wall of which has survived because it was reused for Henry VIII's palace. Note the red brick-work of 1539, put in after the vaults were pulled down.*

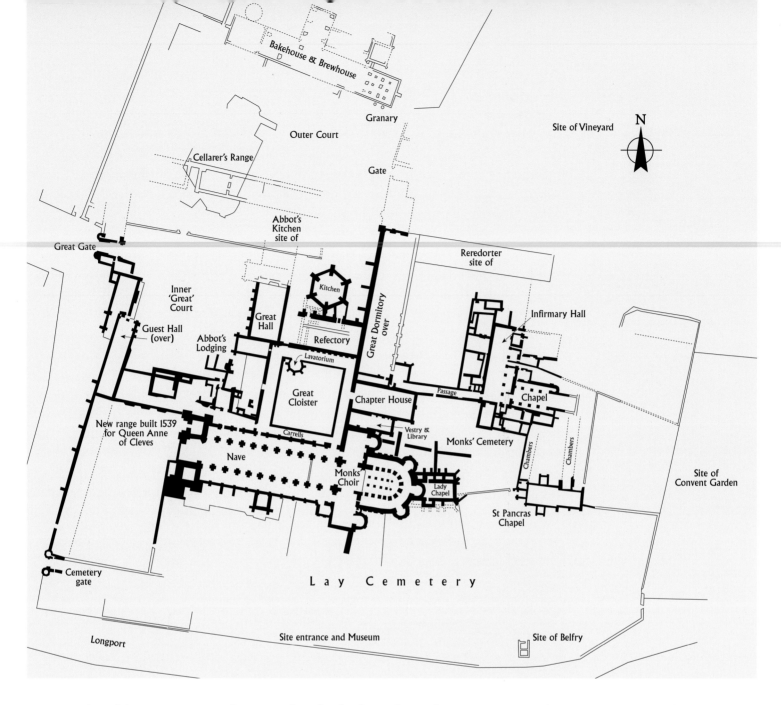

Labels within the plan:

Bakehouse & Brewhouse

Granary

Site of Vineyard

N

Outer Court

Cellarer's Range

Gate

Reredorter site of

Abbot's Kitchen site of

Great Gate

Inner 'Great' Court

Kitchen

Infirmary Hall

Guest Hall (over)

Abbot's Lodging

Great Hall

Refectory

Great Dormitory over

Lavatorium

Great Cloister

Passage

Chapel

Chapter House

Vestry & Library

Monks' Cemetery

Chambers

Chambers

New range built 1539 for Queen Anne of Cleves

Carrells

Nave

Monks' Choir

Lady Chapel

St Pancras Chapel

Site of Convent Garden

Cemetery gate

L a y   C e m e t e r y

Longport

Site entrance and Museum

Site of Belfry

ABOVE: *Plan of the main buildings of St Augustine's Abbey. The cellarer's range, along with the brewhouse and bakehouse to the north, were demolished in 1539, and were only recently rediscovered by means of archaeological excavation.*

rediscovered and rebuilt in the 19th century, it had formed the centre of Henry VIII's royal lodging, built here in 1538–39, immediately after the Dissolution (with a special new range for his new wife, Queen Anne of Cleves). The abbey church and monastic buildings were pulled down, many of the materials being taken in 1540–41 to build the king's new forts on the east Kent coast, and to strengthen the walls of Calais.

Other monastic buildings, such as the infirmary complex to the east, have been excavated and recovered, and we know a great deal about the abbey precinct as a whole, which is still partly surrounded by a high stone wall. The outer courts and the abbey vineyard to the north are now covered by a new teacher training college; the cellarer's garden to the east contains Canterbury prison (built in 1808). On the west side one can still see, from the road, the two magnificent gatehouses: the cemetery gate on the south-west, which faced the Burgate, a main gate into the city, and the superb Great Gate (or Abbot Fyndon Gate), completed in 1308. To the south of the abbey church was the large cemetery for the laypeople, and on the large mound in the south-east corner of the precinct once stood the detached bell-tower, overlooking the Longport street-market.

ABOVE: *View north-west across the cloister garth to the rebuilt abbot's great hall. The roof on the far left covers the early 7th-century archbishops' tombs.*

RIGHT: *Detail of a fine carved and inscribed 12th-century capital in the on-site museum.*

Glastonbury Abbey

GLASTONBURY, SOMERSET

ABOVE: *A view of the 15th-century roof of the abbey's great barn, just outside the precinct.*

RIGHT: *The abbot's kitchen, with its octagonal stone roof, is the only intact building in the precinct.*

This is perhaps the most famous abbey in England; certainly it was once the richest, with a net annual income of over £3,000. When it was dissolved by Henry VIII in 1539, the abbot, Richard Whiting, and two of the monks were hanged on the top of the nearby Tor, and great parts of the huge church and monastic buildings were pulled down. Today the ruins give only a vague impression of its former magnificence, though in the 20th century the site was recovered by the Church, and became a major tourist site. Unlike St Augustine's abbey in Canterbury, whose origins and early history are well documented by the Venerable Bede, Glastonbury's origins are shrouded in myth and legend, and it is only in the later Anglo-Saxon period, in the time of its most famous abbot, St Dunstan (AD 940–57), that its history becomes a little clearer.

The myths start with the arrival in Britain, soon after the death of Christ, of Joseph of Arimathea, and are followed by the legends of the burial of King Arthur and Queen Guinevere. The Christian site at Glastonbury may have been founded by King Ine of Wessex in about AD 705, but it was Dunstan's recreation of a Benedictine monastery here in AD 940 that started Glastonbury on the path to greatness. Dunstan went on to

refound Westminster Abbey and become archbishop of Canterbury, and was certainly the most influential monk in the whole of the Anglo–Saxon period. He died in AD 988.

By the late Anglo–Saxon period there was a considerable monastery here; elements of its buildings have been found by archaeologists, though the investigations undertaken in the earlier part of the 20th century were far from satisfactory. Soon after the Norman Conquest, it was documented as by far the richest abbey in Britain (followed by Ely and Christ Church, Canterbury); however, in contrast to most of the other great English monasteries, we have no direct archaeological evidence for the early Norman rebuilding. A large new church must have been constructed, and may have been complete by about 1120, but this was totally destroyed by fire in 1184. Immediately afterwards, St Mary's chapel, the finest surviving building on the site, was erected. Remarkably, it was built in the late Romanesque mode, with no trace of the transitional Gothic style used at nearby Wells Cathedral or, most famously, at Canterbury. The early Gothic style was used, however, for the late 12th-century great new abbey church, east of St Mary's chapel; frustratingly, only fragmentary ruins now survive of this huge and once magnificent building. The west doorway, a portion of the nave south aisle wall, and parts of the transepts and presbytery do, however, give us some insights. The extreme east end of the church was enlarged in the 14th century, and then given an eastern chapel (the Edgar chapel) in the early 16th century, making the whole church over 580 feet long from end to end.

To the south of the church are traces of the great cloister, the entrance to the chapter house and the refectory undercroft (as well as the reredorter drains) – but little else. To the west, however, the magnificent square abbot's kitchen, with its large stone octagonal roof, does survive, and this is well worth a visit. Further away is the abbey gatehouse on Market Street, and beyond the precinct wall on the south-east is a fine intact great barn. Other Glastonbury abbey barns survive at the nearby manors at Doulting and Pilton.

BELOW: *View across St Mary's (or the Lady) chapel to the western doorway of the main church. Beneath the Lady chapel is the crypt chapel of St Joseph.*

Westminster Abbey

LONDON

HISTORY

- 7th- or 8th-century founding of abbey
- AD 959 Creation of Benedictine abbey
- c.1050 Rebuilding for King Edward the Confessor
- 1540 Dissolution of abbey
- 1560 Foundation of new 'Royal Peculiar', with a dean and chapter
- 1865 rebuilding of chapter house

SPECIAL FEATURES

- Early Norman dormitory undercroft (now museum)
- Great and Little cloisters
- Chapter house, rebuilt mid 13th century
- 12th-century infirmary chapel ruins
- Cellarer's garden, still a garden

ABOVE: *Detail of Giles Gilbert Scott's fine statue of Christ in a quatrefoil above the chapter house doorway.*

RIGHT: *The altar in the late 11th-century 'Pyx Chamber' (in the dormitory undercroft). The boxes, or pyxes, containing samples of the coinage were kept here.*

As with Glastonbury, the beginnings of this famous abbey are obscured by legend. St Peter himself is said to have consecrated this church in the early 7th century (appearing one night just before the bishop of London was to perform the ceremony!). The first monastic settlement was established on an island, Thorney, beside the Thames, at the mouth of the River Tyburn, some time in the middle Anglo-Saxon period. It was no doubt destroyed by the Vikings in the 9th century, but in AD 959 the newly appointed bishop of London, Dunstan, was able to persuade King Edgar to re-establish the monastery along the lines of his own abbey at Glastonbury. There is still a chapel of St Dunstan, on the east side of the later dormitory (now part of Westminster School gymnasium), which may be on the site of the later Anglo-Saxon abbey church.

In the middle of the 11th century the abbey sprang immediately to prominence when it was adopted by King Edward the Confessor (1042–66) and rebuilt on a large scale as a new 'Norman' monastery. The church was dedicated on 28 December 1065, just a few days before King Edward died at the very beginning of 1066. Famously, William the Conqueror was crowned and anointed here on Christmas Day 1066, and since that time nearly every English sovereign has been crowned here.

After the Conquest a series of Norman abbots were appointed and the new royal monastery flourished greatly, becoming the second richest abbey in Britain after

ABOVE: *The late 17th-century arcades of the infirmary (or Little) cloister are on the site of the Norman infirmary hall. The buildings above were rebuilt after bombing had destroyed the earlier ones in 1942.*

PREVIOUS PAGE: *The fine, but worn, mid 14th-century vaults in the south cloister walk, looking east.*

Glastonbury. Remarkably, parts of the early Norman dormitory, reredorter and refectory still survive, and in two passageways between the great cloister and infirmary cloister, one still walks underneath barrel vaults that were constructed in the 1070s. East of the infirmary cloister (or Little cloister), one can see the ruins of the 12th-century infirmary chapel of St Katherine, while the infirmary cloister itself is still partly surrounded by the 14th-century chambers of senior monks, though the arcades were rebuilt in 1680-1.

In 1246 King Henry III started to rebuild the abbey on a colossal scale in the new French Gothic style. In its eastern arm he built a magnificent new shrine to St Edward the Confessor, which still survives. He also completely rebuilt the chapter house as a magnificent octagonal structure. The roof and vaults were destroyed in the 18th century (when the building was used as the Public Record Office), but were magnificently restored by George Gilbert Scott (at government expense) in 1866–72. The chapter house, which still contains its wonderful medieval tiled floor, was used as an early meeting place for Parliament (which later moved to the monks' refectory).

After a great fire in the monastery in 1298, most of the domestic buildings had to be rebuilt. The reconstruction is best seen in the surviving north wall of the refectory, which was heightened and given new windows. The rebuilding of the cloister continued in the 14th century with the installation of magnificent stone vaults. To the south-west (on the Dean's Yard frontage), a new cellarer's range was built, with rib-vaulted undercrofts: parts of these are still used as chapter offices. At its north end, Abbot Litlyngton (1362–86) built himself a magnificent new house, with a kitchen and great hall (still used by Westminster School), and a great chamber, the 'Jerusalem Chamber', which is still

ABOVE: *Pyx Chamber Door.*

RIGHT: *The west front towers were not finished until 1745, but the fine early-Tudor masonry below them was in the process of being built just before the Dissolution.*

used for many important meetings. Attached to it is the early 16th-century Jericho Parlour. All of these buildings are still part of the deanery. To the south of the abbey complex is a large walled garden. This was originally the cellarer's garden, and the stone walls on the east and southern sides are still for the most part the 14th-century ones.

That so much of the medieval fabric of these buildings survived is due to the refoundation of the abbey by Queen Elizabeth I, who installed a new dean and chapter, including some extremely powerful men. Despite suffering serious bomb damage in the Second World War, the buildings to the south of the abbey church are still the most important complex of medieval chambers to survive in the whole of London.

Peterborough Abbey

PETERBOROUGH, CAMBRIDGESHIRE

HISTORY

- AD 655 Foundation of the double 'Minster' of Medeshamstede
- AD 965 Creation of new Benedictine abbey
- 1116 Large fire and start of rebuilding of new abbey church
- 1238 Completion of west front, and dedication of church
- 1539–41 Dissolution of monastery and creation of new bishop, dean and chapter

SPECIAL FEATURES

- Early 13th-century west front, Alwalton marble font and effigies of abbots
- Remains of lavatorium and refectory south of cloister
- Remains of monks' chambers around infirmary hall

ABOVE: *Alwalton marble effigy of one of the early 13th-century abbots of Peterborough.*

RIGHT: *The 15th-century and later clock mechanisms now displayed in the north choir aisle.*

eterborough was the greatest of a series of monasteries founded on the western edge of the Fens in the 7th century. Originally it was called Medeshamstede, and its situation by the River Nene, just before it flows into the peat Fens, has always been a strategic location. The present large town grew up outside the abbey gates in the middle ages and was greatly expanded in the later part of the 20th century. The first monastery was founded by Peada, king of Mercia, in about AD 655, and probably followed the Celtic tradition as a 'double' monastery with communities of both sexes. This would have changed in the later 7th century, when the Roman tradition of St Augustine became dominant in England. In AD 870 the monastery was destroyed by the Vikings and was then abandoned. Only in the later 10th century was it revived as a new Benedictine foundation by Æthelwold, bishop of Winchester (and colleague of St Dunstan). He started to rebuild the abbey of St Peter in AD 965, and in AD 972, with royal support, it was reconsecrated. The abbey and town were now surrounded by a strong fortification; hence the name, conferred later, of the 'burh' (borough) of St Peter. The late Anglo-Saxon abbots opposed the Norman invaders (Abbot Leofric died at the battle of Hastings), and the new King William installed a Norman knight, Turold, as abbot. After a difficult period the abbey's fortunes revived, and by the time of Domesday Book it was the eleventh richest abbey in England. Its history through this period is well recorded in the abbey's own version of the Anglo-Saxon Chronicle.

The late Anglo-Saxon abbey church survived until burnt out in a great fire in 1116, and traces of this church have been found below the present south transept. Work on the present very large

Romanesque abbey church was started in 1118, and the presbytery and monks' choir were ready to be consecrated by the bishop of Lincoln, Alexander, in 1140. The very long nave was not completed until the time of Abbot Benedict (1177–94), who was a monk at Canterbury when Archbishop Thomas Becket was murdered in 1170, and brought various Becket relics to Peterborough to attract new pilgrims. The wonderful west front, which is covered in the local marble from Alwalton, was a final addition of the early 13th century. The building still contains a beautiful font and several effigies of abbots from the late 12th and early 13th centuries, all in Alwalton marble.

BELOW: J.L. Pearson's choir stalls of c.1890 on the site of the monks' choir. To the east can be seen the apsidal east end to the sanctuary, built in the early 12th century.

ABOVE: *The fine 15th-century lavatorium in the south cloister walk, where the monks washed their hands before going into the refectory. Sadly, the wash basins have been removed.*

To the south of the abbey church are the remains of several of the monastic buildings, though much that once surrounded the great cloister has sadly been destroyed. The north wall of the refectory is still visible, as is its 13th-century principal doorway on the west; it was flanked by the lavatorium, rebuilt in the 15th century. South-east of the cloister are the impressive remains of the infirmary hall and chapel, dating from the later 13th century. As at Canterbury and Ely, the side aisles were later filled in with various monks' chambers, which subsequently led to their preservation after the Dissolution. To the north of the infirmary, the infirmarer's lodging and table hall (where meat could be eaten) have also survived. The last abbot, John Chambers (1528–39), became the first bishop in 1541, so his house, south-west of the cloister, survives in part as the bishop's palace. There is a fine early 13th-century gateway to the abbot's house near the west front; beyond it to the west is the late 12th-century principal outer gate to the monastery, built by Abbot Benedict and rebuilt in the early 14th century. Beside it are the remains of the chapel of St Thomas Becket (now the tea-room). Beyond is the busy market place of the old and new town.

Bury St Edmunds Abbey

BURY ST EDMUNDS, SUFFOLK

HISTORY

- AD 633 Founding of the first church by St Sigebert
- AD 869 Murder of King Edmund
- 1020 Founding of Benedictine abbey
- 1081 Start of work on huge new church
- 1327 Great riots
- 1539 Dissolution and demolition of abbey

SPECIAL FEATURES

- Ruins of great church, crypt and monastic buildings
- 12th-century Tower of St James
- 14th-century Great Gate Tower
- 13th-century abbot's bridge and neighbouring precinct wall
- Ruins of 12th-century west front with later houses built into it

ABOVE: *The abbot's bridge, which also carries the precinct boundary wall over the River Lark.*

RIGHT: *The view to the south-east, across the great eastern crypt of the abbey church.*

At the centre of the busy west Suffolk market town of Bury is a largely 'green' rectangular monastic precinct that once contained one of the largest medieval churches in England. Sadly, all that remains today of this huge building, once about 500 feet long– including its large eastern crypt – are ruined fragments in a garden. After the Dissolution the church was provisionally earmarked by Henry VIII for a new cathedral, but the plan came to nothing and the abbey was demolished.

The site, originally called Beodricesworth, was first given a Christian community by Sigebert, king of the East Angles, in AD 633. In AD 903 the remains of King Edmund, martyred by the Danes in AD 869, were brought here to the church of a community of secular priests. Only in 1020 were the priests replaced by a group of 20 Benedictine monks, who then ran an increasingly important royal abbey, with many pilgrims coming to the shrine of St Edmund, king and martyr. As at Peterborough, the fortified monastery town (a burh) came to be known by the saint's name, St Edmundsbury; and as at St Augustine's abbey in Canterbury, a new round building was put up to contain the royal relics in the late Anglo–Saxon period. In the years immediately after the Norman Conquest Abbot Baldwin (1065–97) made plans to build a new Norman abbey. The

ABOVE: *The well-preserved Great Gateway to the abbey, solidly built in* c.1330 *and heightened in* c.1360.

large new eastern arm, with a crypt, ambulatory and apsidal eastern chapels (a bigger version of St Augustine's eastern arm) was started in the 1080s and completed by 1095, when the relics of St Edmund were translated to a new shrine. In 1081 a scheme had been launched to turn the abbey into a new cathedral, but this lapsed after 1095 when Norwich got the new bishop's *cathedra* for East Anglia. During the next half-century or so, the two rival monasteries competed with each other, and with Ely, in constructing very long naves and elaborate western transepts; and it is ironic that the largest of these, at Bury, was the only one neither to become a cathedral nor to survive.

To the north of the great church was a large cloister, surrounded by all the principal monastic buildings: only fragments of these now remain, particularly on the northeast, where the chapter house, infirmary and prior's house were situated. The abbot's house was positioned further north; this survived until the early 18th century, when it was demolished.

The finest surviving buildings at the abbey are the two magnificent gatehouses on the west. The early Norman 'Tower of St James', built by Abbot Anselm (1120–48), was both a gatehouse and a belfry to the neighbouring church of St James. Ironically, it was this latter church which became a cathedral in the 20th century and has now just received its own new tower. The other gatehouse, to the north, is the even more splendid Great Gate, built in the 14th century as the most grandiose element in the refortification of the abbey precinct that followed serious riots in 1327. In this episode, the townspeople managed to break into the abbey, sack it, and set it on fire; several monks were murdered, and a huge amount of damage was done. The town was heavily fined, but turmoil erupted again in the Peasants' Revolt of 1381. The citizens of Bury longed to break free of the abbey's control, but this was only finally achieved at the Dissolution in 1539.

RIGHT: *View west from the ruins of the north transept of the great church, to the brand new tower on St Edmundsbury Cathedral. In the foreground is the site of the round church, built in 1020 to house the relics of St Edmund.*

Abingdon Abbey

ABINGDON, OXFORDSHIRE

The first religious community to take up residence beside the Thames at Abingdon probably arrived there in the later 7th century under the patronage of the royal house of Wessex. The early history, is, however, much obscured by later legends, and it is not until about AD 954, and the arrival of St Æthelwold as abbot, that Abingdon comes into focus again as one of the most important of the new Benedictine monasteries. Some fragments of what may have been Æthelwold's church were discovered beneath the very large Norman excavations in 1922; it is probable that he had created a flourishing new monastery here

ABOVE: *A 15th-century corbelled head adorns the gatehouse.*

RIGHT: *View through the late 15th-century abbey gatehouse, with the church of St Nicholas on the left. The right-hand gateway arch was built in the 19th century.*

ABOVE: *The Checker as viewed from the north-west, with its 13th-century chimney stack and wind vents, a very rare survival.*

before moving on to take up the post of bishop of Winchester in AD 963. After the Norman Conquest, Abbot Reinald (1084–96) built the eastern arm of a large new church, and this building was completed by Abbot Faritius (1100–17). Unfortunately, this building was completely obliterated after the Dissolution in 1538, and only foundations (briefly exposed in 1922) remain. Burials to the north of the church were also uncovered in a 1989 archaeological excavation, along with the base of an octagonal bell-tower.

The buildings that do survive from the monastery are the gatehouse range on the west, and a guest house and service buildings on the south. The fine late 15th-century gatehouse has a medieval foot passage and smaller gate to the north, balanced in the 19th century by the addition of another foot passage to the south. To the north of the gate is the late 12th-century church of St Nicholas, whose west door faces on to the market place. The 15th-century chancel attached to the gateway is just inside the abbey precinct. South of the gatehouse was the 12th-century Hospital of St John, with the almonry beyond it. All these buildings were preserved after the Dissolution, and were used after 1556 by the newly founded Borough of Abingdon for courts and council offices.

Along the south side of the abbey a millstream was created, perhaps before the Conquest, and beside this, and close to the mill itself, are a range of buildings which included the bakehouse and granary. Next to them on the east is a building now called the Checker, and the Long Gallery. The latter was originally a series of first-floor guest chambers, with a long, narrow passage running along outside them; later all the internal partitions were removed. The Checker is a fine 13th-century stone building on a rib-vaulted undercroft, with large upper chambers entered from an external stair. This may also have been an earlier guest house; rebuilt in the 14th century, it still has its fine 13th-century fireplace, with the original tall chimney flue above it and, at the top of this, groups of three miniature stepped lancets that act as wind vents. This is a very rare survival indeed in England.

Muchelney Abbey

MUCHELNEY, SOMERSET

HISTORY

- AD 693 Founding of monastery
- AD 939 Refoundation by King Athelstan
- Early 12th century – new church and monastic buildings erected
- 1538 Dissolution and destruction of the monastery
- 1872 First excavation of the site

SPECIAL FEATURES

- Foundations of 12th-century church and cloister
- Remains of Anglo-Saxon church below later monks' choir
- Well-preserved abbot's great chamber, kitchen and stairs

ABOVE: *View of the parish church from one of the abbot's rooms above the south cloister walk, built by Abbot Thomas Broke.*

RIGHT: *The abbot's house as seen from the south, with the blind tracery in his great hall on the right.*

I n the southern Somerset levels, formerly areas of marshland and water, are a series of islands, several of which housed Anglo-Saxon monastic sites. The most famous is probably Athelney, which was refounded by King Alfred. A few miles south-east of Athelney is Muchelney (the 'big island' in Anglo-Saxon), which lies in the marshes just south of Langport and Huish Episcopi. This island was 'difficult of access', to quote the 12th-century historian William of Malmesbury, 'and in summer may be reached by foot or, more often, by horse, but in winter never'.

The monastery here was perhaps first founded by King Ine of Wessex (688–726) in the later 7th century, but the surviving charter 'proving' this was in fact forged at a later date. It was refounded in the early 10th century, probably after Viking attacks had destroyed it, and the apsidal church in the deep archaeological excavations at the centre of the site may well be the remains of the 10th-century church. By this time it had become a reformed Benedictine foundation, and in AD 995 it was called a 'little monastery' (probably in relation to the very large new monastery at nearby Glastonbury). After the Norman Conquest, a large new Norman church was built with an eastern ambulatory and a series of semicircular apsidal chapels. South of this church was the usual cloister, with the chapter house, dormitory, refectory, etc. around it. All

these buildings were demolished soon after the Dissolution in 1538, and all that we see today are the foundations that were re-exposed in 1873. These do, however, give us the whole plan of the core of the monastery. They also show us how the church was enlarged on the east in the 13th century, with a new Lady Chapel and other flanking chapels. The chapter house was also enlarged, as was the monks' reredorter (latrine) on the south, and by the early 14th century there may have been about 50 monks here. After the Black Death the numbers dropped rapidly, and at the Dissolution there were only ten.

BELOW: *South-west corner of the cloister, with door into the abbot's house. The cloister was rebuilt to include a fan vault in the early 16th century.*

In the late middle ages, however, Muchelney was still a rich monastery, and this is well shown by the buildings that survived the Dissolution, notably the abbot's lodging on the south side of the cloister. As at many monasteries (e.g. nearby Forde Abbey), the abbot was an important local landowner who, like a secular lord, needed to live in a grand house. In the later 15th century he completely rebuilt his lodging at Muchelney, turning the refectory into his great hall, flanked on the west by his fine kitchen (still roofed), and a grand stair leading up to the abbot's great chamber on the first floor. Here, the elegant fireplace (which probably had a picture over it) still remains, as do good traceried windows on the south. These still contain some original stained glass in their heads, with the initials of Abbot Thomas Broke (1505–22). The south cloister walk was rebuilt, with a fan vault, in Abbot Broke's time, and above this are several fine chambers, which belonged to the abbot's house. After the Dissolution the abbey became the property of Edward Seymour, Earl of Hertford (1500–52), who became 'the Protector' Duke of Somerset under Edward VI. At this time the abbot's house was converted into a tenants' farmhouse, and it remained thus until 1927, when it officially became an ancient monument. To the west, some of the farm buildings still remain, including the barns that belonged to the almonry. North of the abbey is the parish church, its churchyard cross, and the early 14th-century vicar's house.

St Alban's Abbey

ST ALBANS, HERTFORDSHIRE

ABOVE: *St Alban's Abbey church as seen from the south-west, showing the remains of the early 14th-century north cloister walk.*

RIGHT: *View through the late 14th-century arches of the great gateway.*

All that is left of the once huge and powerful Abbey of St Alban, known for a time as the 'premier abbey of England', is the vast abbey church (which became a cathedral only in 1877) and the very large three–storied gatehouse immediately to the west of the abbey. All the medieval monastic buildings, which lay to the south of these two structures, were demolished after the Dissolution; all that remain of them today are humps and bumps in the grass. Various excavations have taken place here, and in 1978 the very large chapter house was fully excavated before a modern building was built on top of it. To the west of this, the blind arcading on the north side of the north cloister walk can still be seen on the outside of the nave south aisle.

The great medieval abbey, the fourth richest in England at the time of the Dissolution, lies on a hillside to the north–east of the river Ver. Immediately to the south–west of the river is the site of the once large Roman town of Verulamium. St Alban was probably a 3rd–century inhabitant of this town who sheltered a Christian priest in his house, and then himself became a Christian. For this he was taken out of the town, across the river and up the hill on the other side, where he was executed. All of this is told to us by the

ABOVE: *The huge main gate-house to the abbey, viewed from inside the former monastic precincts. This structure survived the Dissolution because it became the town jail and courthouse in 1553. In 1871 the grammar school was moved here from the Lady chapel.*

early 8th-century historian Bede, who goes on to say that 'a beautiful church worthy of his martyrdom was built here, where sick folk are healed and frequent miracles take place to this day'. Excavations undertaken so far have not found this church. The present very large abbey church was begun after the Norman Conquest in 1077 by Paul, the nephew of the famous Benedictine abbot Lanfranc, who became archbishop of Canterbury in 1070. Paul used the ruins of the old Roman town as his quarry, and one can still see much Roman brick in the Norman parts of the church, though inside it is still largely covered in plaster. In 1154, Abbot Robert de Gorron (1151–66) was acknowledged the premier abbot of England, a rather empty title, because of the foundation's supposed very early beginnings in the Roman period. By the end of the 12th century there were nearly 100 monks here; the nave had been lengthened, and a beautiful west front was going up. Traces of this, with superb carved Purbeck marble, can still be seen behind the late Victorian west porch. (Externally the abbey church, particularly the transepts and west front, suffered greatly during the very expensive and destructive late 19th-century restoration campaigns under Lord Grimthorpe.)

During the 13th and 14th centuries the abbey flourished. Matthew Paris was a monk here when he wrote his renowned Chronicles, and the abbacy was held by a series of great men, including Richard of Wallingford (1327–36), famous for his astronomical clock, and the greatest of them all, Thomas de la Mere (1349–96). Thereafter the status of the abbey declined; at the end of its life Cardinal Wolsey was abbot *in commendam* (1521–30), but probably never visited it. The abbey was dissolved on 5 December 1539, and three years later the great church, by now 550 feet long, was sold to the mayor and burgesses of the town. It is to them that we owe the survival of this fine building.

Lindisfarne Priory

LINDISFARNE, NORTHUMBERLAND

HISTORY

- AD 635 Founding of monastery by Aidan
- AD 687 St Cuthbert buried here
- AD 793 Sacked by Vikings
- Late 11th century – New priory church built
- 13th–14th centuries – Claustral buildings and prior's house
- 1537 Priory dissolved

SPECIAL FEATURES

- Ruins of fine Norman priory church
- Ruins of east and west cloister ranges
- Remains of large, fortified prior's house
- Anglo–Saxon parish church of St Mary to the west

ABOVE: *View north-east across the ruins from the monks' kitchen. The priory church is in the background, with the western towers on the left.*

Holy Island is a remarkable place. Situated just off the Northumbrian coast only a few miles from the Scottish border at Berwick–upon–Tweed, it is still accessible overland only by a causeway at low tide. In AD 635 the missionary bishop from Iona, Aidan, arrived on this island, given to him by King Oswald, and established his see at a new monastery here. The foundation rapidly flourished; at the time of its most famous bishop, Cuthbert (685–7) – who was buried here after dying on the nearby Inner Farne Island – the monks were making one of the greatest masterpieces of 7th–century art, the Lindisfarne Gospels (now in the British Library). Because of its exposed position and fine natural harbour, the monastery was one of the first places in England to be sacked by the Vikings, who attacked on 7 June 793. The monastery struggled on, but in AD 875 it was finally abandoned, and the monks took refuge on the mainland, taking with them the

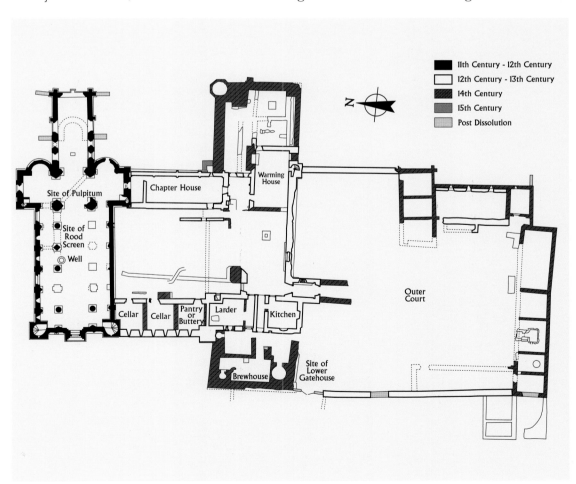

ABOVE: *The nave of the priory church looking north-east with its famous rainbow arch – one surviving diagonal now spanning the crossing.*

body of St Cuthbert. In AD 882 they settled at Chester–le–Street, but a century later their successors moved to the much more secure site at Durham during the renewed attack of the Vikings in AD 995. Nothing has yet been excavated of the famous Anglo–Saxon monastery at Lindisfarne, but it must have been close to the later church. Some fine Anglo–Saxon crosses and gravestones can, however, be seen in the museum.

After the Norman Conquest the Durham community briefly took refuge on Lindisfarne in 1069–70 (even taking the coffin of St Cuthbert back with them), but the monks soon returned to Durham, where a major new Benedictine monastery was founded at the cathedral in 1083. The sacred site at Holy Island, which now belonged to the prior and convent of Durham, was made into a cell of the new monastery, and a small priory was established there. The surviving ruined church was built here at the end of the 11th century: in some ways it is a miniature Durham Cathedral. Originally it had three apses at the east end, but in the mid 12th century a larger, square-ended, chancel was built. The building had early rib-vaults throughout, again as at the cathedral, and traces of these can be seen in the upper walls, and especially in the remaining diagonal rib that spans the crossing.

In the 13th century small-scale monastic buildings were built around a cloister on the south side of the church, with a cellarer's range on the west and the smaller chapter house on the east (with perhaps the dormitory above). To the south was the refectory, with a kitchen and larder on the west. The south range was lengthened and strengthened at the end of the 14th century, to guard against attacks by the Scots. By this time, a large prior's house had been incorporated into the building. Beyond was the walled outer court with a gatehouse. Immediately to the west of the priory church is the parish church of St Mary; though rebuilt in the late 13th century, it contains elements of an earlier pre-Conquest church that may date back to the 10th or early 11th century. It is also thought fragments of the 7th century church may have been incorporated.

CATHEDRAL PRIORIES
(Benedictines)

The English cathedral priories were an extremely rich and powerful group of Benedictine monasteries that had the bishop as titular abbot. His deputy, the prior, effectively ran the monastery. Many of these priors became very important figures in their own right, wearing mitres and sitting in the House of Lords.

After the Dissolution, all of the cathedral priories were refounded, with new deans and chapters, so that many of the monastic buildings were retained and converted to new uses. Canterbury still has the largest collection of monastic buildings (and ruins) in Britain, and Ely has a uniquely well-preserved prior's chapel. At Durham, the large late medieval dormitory and the priory kitchen have survived, while at Worcester the unique circular chapter house is a great rarity. With great cathedrals at the cores of these institutions, they are some of the most visited monasteries in England.

ABOVE: *An early 13th-century corbelled head of a Benedictine monk (made of Purbeck marble) in the choir at Rochester.*

BELOW: *St Swithun's Priory, Winchester. North-west view of the priory stabling in the outer court near the entrance gate.*

Christ Church Priory

CANTERBURY, KENT

ABOVE: *The ruins of the south arcade of the early Norman Infirmary Hall.*

RIGHT: *The round 12th-century water tower in the infirmary cloister, with the chapter house and the monks' night passage (all re-roofed in the 14th century) behind it.*

Throughout St Dunstan's time as archbishop of Canterbury (959–88) the city had only one Benedictine monastery, at St Augustine's abbey; indeed, it was St Dunstan who reconstructed this abbey in AD 978 and gave it new life. Not long after his death, however, the secular community at his cathedral, which lay inside the Roman city walls, was replaced by a group of Benedictine monks, and in the early 11th century the cathedral was greatly enlarged on the west and given a cloister. In 1070 the Norman conqueror King William brought to Canterbury as his new archbishop an eminent Italian Benedictine monk called Lanfranc, who had been abbot of William's own monastery in Caen. With him came a group of monks who were to rebuild the monastic houses of England. Lanfranc immediately started to rebuild his own cathedral, and before his death in 1089 large new monastic buildings had been completed around a cloister on the north side of the cathedral nave. Particularly impressive was the great first–floor dormitory, large sections of which still survive: it was built to house up to 150 monks, and hence to be the largest monastery in England.

ABOVE: *View north-west across the early 15th-century cloister to the archbishop's palace. The monks' lavatorium was in the two open arches on the right.*

OPPOSITE: *The mid 12th-century monumental staircase to the North Hall. The four main pillars at the base of the stairs were built to support another large water tank.*

The next archbishop, Anselm, an even more famous Benedictine monk, oversaw the addition of a vast new monks' choir and sanctuary to the east end of the cathedral. Soon afterwards an equally large infirmary hall and chapel (260 feet long) were added on the north–eastern side. The whole monastic precinct, within the north–east part of the walled city, was also greatly enlarged, and by the time Archbishop Thomas Becket was murdered in 1170 there was a very large complex of buildings extending eastwards and northwards from the cathedral. Parts of many of these buildings still survive, including the great gatehouse and north hall on the north–west, and the brewhouse and bakehouse range on the north. The core of the monastery had also been rebuilt, with a second dormitory and infirmary cloister to the east of the great dormitory. This still contains 12th–century structures such as the circular water–tower and the east cloister arcade (the only ones to survive *in situ* in England).

Not only was the Benedictine priory at Canterbury the largest in the country, it is also the best documented, and has the best collection of surviving monastic buildings anywhere in Britain. Many of these were rebuilt during the later Middle Ages, especially under priors Henry of Eastry (1285–1331) and Thomas Chillenden (1391–1411), and even after the Dissolution in 1540 the new dean and chapter kept and adapted many of them. Even the communal buildings, like the great dormitory, refectory, kitchen and infirmary, were initially only unroofed, and parts of the ruined walls of these buildings have survived.

Inside the cathedral, the huge monks' choir and the shrine of St Thomas Becket (rebuilt

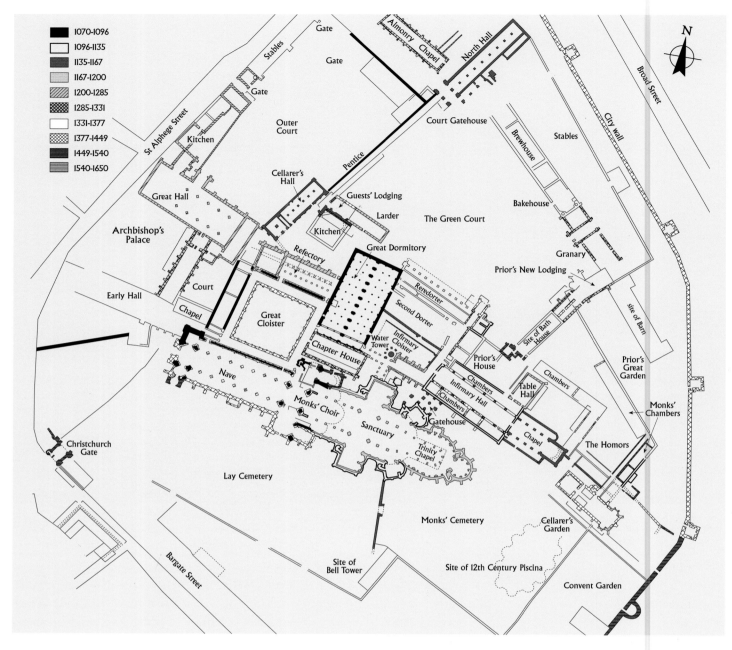

after a great fire in 1174) are justly famous; immediately outside the cathedral, the vaulted cloister (rebuilt in the early 15th century) is also a superb structure. North of the chapter house are a late 11th–century groin–vaulted passageway, which connects the two cloisters, and a 12th–century first–floor 'night passage' that ran from the dormitory to the choir. The latter was heightened in the late 14th century, and given a new roof and windows. Beyond this can be seen the ruins of the very long reredorter, with a late 14th–century gatehouse on its north side. This gate leads out into the 'Green Court', originally the great outer court-yard to the priory. On its eastern side is the deanery, which still contains large sections of the monks' bathhouse and prior's 'New Lodging'. On the north side of the Green Court are the remains of the brewhouse, bakehouse, granary and stables. To the north–west is the great 12th–century gatehouse, already mentioned; connecting this with the inner gateway to the kitchen, larder and guest lodgings was a 15th–century timber–framed covered pas-sageway called the 'pentice' (part of it still survives). West of the boundary wall and behind the pentice is a large separate precinct containing the archbishop's palace.

ABOVE: *View west down the north cloister walk. The heraldry on the vaults is one of the largest collections of medieval heraldry in Britain.*

RIGHT: *The Christ Church gateway, the principal entry into the cathedral precincts, was completed in 1517, and has early Renaissance, as well as late Gothic, decoration.*

St Swithun's Priory

WINCHESTER, HAMPSHIRE

HISTORY

- AD 648 First cathedral built
- AD 964 Founding of new Benedictine monastery by Bishop Æthelwold
- 1079 Start of new cathedral and monastic buildings
- 1539 Dissolution of priory

SPECIAL FEATURES

- Enormous cathedral church
- Remains of 11th-century chapter house
- 15th-century prior's house with 13th-century porch
- Outer court stables, guest house and gateway

ABOVE: *Illuminated letter from the Winchester Bible, showing Bishop Henry of Blois, who was also the abbot of Glastonbury.*

RIGHT: *The beautiful 13th-century vaulted porch to the prior's house (now the deanery).*

 Christian church was first built in the middle of the ruined Roman city of Winchester in about AD 648 for St Birinus, after he was given the site by Cenwalh, king of the West Saxons. Soon afterwards Birinus became the first bishop of the West Saxons, and over the next four centuries this cathedral was rebuilt and enlarged several times, as the large-scale excavations carried out in the 1960s showed. The most important of the later Anglo-Saxon bishops was St Æthelwold (963–84), who expelled the old secular priests from the cathedral and brought in a new community of Benedictine monks from his old monastery at Abingdon, where he had been a great reforming abbot. In AD 971 he set up a new shrine to one of his predecessors as bishop, Swithun, making him the most famous of all bishops of Winchester. In the later Anglo-Saxon period the cathedral also became the burial place of many kings of Wessex and England (though not of King Alfred): the most famous of these was Cnut (d. 1035), who was also king of Denmark and Norway. Their bones lie in wooden mortuary chests, which can still be seen on top of the stone screens beside the cathedral's high altar.

After the Norman Conquest one of the king's chaplains, Walkelin, was made bishop of Winchester (1070–98). He considered replacing the monks with a new body of canons, but in the event this did not happen, and in 1079 Walkelin started to build a

ABOVE: *The main gateway into the priory on the south is still the modern entrance to the close. The late medieval stables can be glimpsed through the gateway.*

ABOVE RIGHT: *The magnificent late 11th-century arcade on the west side of the chapter house is made of Quarr stone from the Isle of Wight, but incorporating three huge shafts of Bath stone. Above it is the south transept of the cathedral.*

vast new cathedral (534 feet long, and larger than anything in France at that date) for his monks. He even appointed his brother Simeon prior of the monastery. By April 1093 the eastern arm was complete, enabling the monks to leave the old Anglo–Saxon cathedral, which was destroyed soon afterwards. At the same time, large new monastic buildings were put up around a new cloister on the south. Unfortunately, most of these, along with the cloister, were destroyed after the Dissolution; but the splendid early Norman western arcade of the chapter house is still visible.

By the mid 12th century the cathedral, with a large pair of western towers, was complete, as were the monastic buildings. The bishop was the immensely powerful Cluniac monk Henry of Blois (1129–71), the brother of King Stephen (1135–54), and also abbot at Glastonbury. The wonderful Winchester Bible and the black Tournai font in the nave date from his time.

In the later middle ages much rebuilding work was done at the cathedral, particularly under Bishop William of Wykeham (1366–1404), and many of the monastic buildings must also have been rebuilt. Unfortunately, much rebuilding was also done after the medieval period, so that few of them survive. One can, however, see remains of the monks' kitchen and cellarer's vaulted undercroft on the south–west side of the cloister, as well as the magnificent prior's house (today the deanery) to the south–east. There is a very fine 13th–century porch to the latter, and inside a splendid 15th–century prior's hall. In the outer court to the south there is still a fine guest house (now called the Pilgrims' Hall) with an early hammer–beam roof, dating from the beginning of the 14th century. Not far away is the main gateway to the priory, just inside which stands a timber–framed stable block that was built in the late 15th century.

St Mary's Priory

WORCESTER, WORCESTERSHIRE

HISTORY

- *c.*AD 670 Foundation of first cathedral church
- AD 983 New Benedictine monastery created for Oswald
- 1084 Start of work on new Norman cathedral and priory
- 1539 Dissolution of priory

SPECIAL FEATURES

- Fine late 14th-century cloister walks
- Large refectory on Norman undercroft
- Unique circular chapter house
- Great gatehouse (Edgar Tower)
- Watergate by River Severn
- Ruins of 'Guesten Hall'

ABOVE: *Some fine late 14th-century angel bosses on the vault of the north cloister walk.*

RIGHT: *The ruined west wall of the Guesten Hall, with the south-east transept of the cathedral behind it.*

T he cathedral church at Worcester was first built in the late 7th century on a high bank overlooking the River Severn, but very little is known of it. In AD 961, however, Archbishop Dunstan rec–ommended to King Edgar that Oswald, a Benedictine monk, should be made bishop of Worcester. Oswald introduced a new monastic community to the cathedral and created several other monasteries in the area (Westbury–on–Trym, Evesham and Pershore). He also created a monastery at Ramsey (in the Fens), and in AD 972 became archbishop of York as well as bishop of Worcester. When he died in AD 992, his tomb in Worcester Cathedral quickly became a shrine. The new monastery at Worcester then became an important centre of learning, but it suffered a setback when sacked by King Harthacnut in 1041.

At about this time there was a young monk at Worcester called Wulfstan. A few years afterwards he became prior, and then, in 1062, bishop. Remarkably, he quickly submitted to William the Conqueror after the Battle of Hastings, and remained throughout his reign the only Anglo–Saxon bishop in England. He also supported

Archbishop Lanfranc's reforms of the church, and Worcester now became attached to Canterbury rather than York. In 1084 Wulfstan started to rebuild his cathedral in the Norman style, and the very fine Norman crypt, with its forest of cushion capitals, is his lasting legacy. After Wulfstan died in 1095, his tomb also quickly became a shrine, but he was not formally canonized until 1203. After this the shrines of Saints Oswald and Wulfstan were put on either side of the high altar, and King John asked to be buried here in 1216. The rebuilding of the eastern arm of the cathedral, with a fine new Lady chapel beyond the high altar, followed in the later 13th century.

BELOW: *The north-west corner of the cloister garth, with the windows of the library above the nave south aisle.*

The monastic buildings were all rebuilt from the end of the 11th century, and squeezed in between the cathedral on the north and the castle to the south. The castle was held for the king by Bishop Wulfstan against rebels in 1074 and 1088. In the 13th century the monks were able to enlarge the precinct and expand on to the castle site. The fine vaulted cloister (rebuilt from the late 14th century) still survives, with the ruins of the great dormitory and reredorter beyond it to the west. On the eastern side of the cloister is Worcester's unique circular chapter house, built early in the 12th century (see picture on page 2). Recent excavations have revealed that there was originally a semicircular passageway running around the eastern and southern sides of the chapter house. The only parallel to this is the slightly later passageway built by Abbot Aelred around the chapter house at Rievaulx. As at Rievaulx, the passageway was demolished in the late 14th century, and replaced by buttresses and new large windows. On the south side of the cloister the 14th-century monks' refectory also remains intact, still sitting on its vaulted 12th-century undercroft; in the east wall of the refectory, above the high table, is a magnificent (but mutilated) 13th-century figure of Christ in Majesty set in an elongated quatrefoil. This fine room is now part of the King's School, as is much of the outer court area of the priory to the south. Traces of the monastic buildings can be found here, but of greatest interest is the 1378 Watergate on to the Severn on the west, and the 1368 great gate (now called the 'Edgar Tower') on the east. North-west of this was the prior's house and 'Guesten Hall', as it was called. Sadly, this is now a ruin: its magnificent roof was taken off in 1859 and can now be seen rebuilt (or close to) at the Avoncroft Museum of Buildings at Bromsgrove.

St Cuthbert's Priory

DURHAM, COUNTY DURHAM

ABOVE: *The Conduit House in the Outer Court, rebuilt in 1751 in an early Gothic Revival style.*

RIGHT: *The huge new monks' dormitory, with its 14th-century roof, which is now the new library and museum.*

Durham is most famous for housing the body of St Cuthbert (brought here in AD 995) in its great Norman cathedral. Soon after the arrival of the relics, a large 'White Church' was built to house them (dedicated on 4 September 998), and this no doubt stood near the present cathedral nave in a strongly defended enclosure. After the Conquest, the first Norman bishop, Walcher of Lorraine (1071–80), built a castle at the neck of the peninsula, and then started to construct a new group of monastic buildings for a community of reformed monks he was intending to bring here. These plans came to an end when he was murdered in Gateshead; but in 1083 his successor as bishop, William of St Calais

(1081–96), brought in 23 Benedictine monks from Monkwearmouth and Jarrow. Five years after this, the bishop was sent into exile for plotting against the new king, William Rufus. He returned in 1091, and the following year he knocked down the nearly 100-year-old 'White Church' and prepared to build a vast new one. The foundations were laid on 7 August 1093, and by 1133 the whole of the magnificent Norman church we see today was complete, with all its new monastic buildings around a cloister to the south. Most of these buildings survive, though many of them were rebuilt, or altered, in the latter middle ages. Outside the southeast corner of the cloister, which later became the prior's lodging (and is still the deanery today), there are traces of the earliest Norman dormitory undercroft and reredorter. In the 12th century the dormitory was removed to the upper part of the west range, and then rebuilt, on a large scale (it is 194 feet long), in 1398–1404. This magnificent building is now the library; it sits on a fine vaulted undercroft, now used as the treasury and restaurant. The south cloister range also has an early Norman vaulted undercroft with above it the monks' refectory. This was converted in about 1680 into a library (now called the Old Library), but much remains of the medieval building, including the serving hatch, the earlier fireplace and the tiled floors, which are below the present raised timber floor. South-west of the refectory is the wonderful octagonal priory kitchen (now a bookshop), which was built, with its very fine rib-vaulted roof, in 1366–74. Sadly, the apsidal east end of the chapter house was demolished in 1796, but it was rebuilt on its original plan in 1895. In the centre of the floor lie many of the grave slabs of the early priors. South of the chapter house are the remains of the monks' prison, and beyond it the very fine prior's house. The first-floor level houses the prior's hall and great chamber, while to the south-east can be seen the remains of the 13th-century prior's chapel. Inside it are remains of superb wall paintings of the late 15th century, showing scenes from the life of the Virgin Mary. To the south of all these buildings is the outer court of the priory, with the principal gatehouse on the east. Several of the medieval buildings around the outer court survive, converted into canons' houses after the Dissolution.

BELOW: *The prior's lodging (now the deanery), south-east of the cloister, with the remains of its 13th-century chapel on the right. Behind is the roof of the eastern arm of the cathedral.*

St Andrew's Priory

ROCHESTER, KENT

ABOVE: *The cowled head of a Benedictine monk, carved in Purbeck marble. It is on a corbel in the monks' choir.*

One of the monks from Rome who came to England with St Augustine in AD 596, Justus, was consecrated the first bishop of Rochester in AD 604 (his tomb can still be seen at St Augustine's abbey in Canterbury). He built a church, which was rediscovered under the north-west corner of the present cathedral in 1889, and built up a small community within the old Roman walled city of Rochester. Its two most famous early bishops were St Paulinus (d. AD 644: a former bishop of York, and apostle of Northumbria) and St Ithamar (d. AD 655: and the first native English bishop). After the Norman Conquest, the remains of these two men were translated to two new shrines on either side of the high altar. The community at Rochester suffered much from the Viking incursions in the mid 9th and early 11th centuries, and at the time of the Norman Conquest the cathedral was at a low ebb. However, everything changed in 1077 with the arrival of Gundulf, a Norman monk who had just assisted Archbishop Lanfranc to rebuild his cathedral in Canterbury. Gundulf came to Rochester both as its diocesan bishop and as a suffragan bishop to Lanfranc. Between them, Lanfranc and Gundulf had decided that Rochester should have not only a new cathedral, but also a new Benedictine monastery beside it. The rebuilding of the cathedral quickly got under way in the 1080s, and the groin-vaulted western part of the crypt dates from this time. A new body of monks was introduced from Canterbury in 1083 (the same year that Durham received its monks), and by the time of Gundulf's death in 1108 there were 60 monks here.

In 1114 Ernulf, another Norman monk, became bishop. He had previously been prior of Christ Church, Canterbury (1096–1107) and then abbot of Peterborough (1107–14). At Rochester he created a large new cloister south-east of the cathedral (positioned here because the site was so restricted), with around it the chapter house, dormitory, refectory and cellarer's range. The chapter house still survives, albeit now without a roof, as does the west wall of the dormitory undercroft. Both buildings were refaced after a fire in 1137: unusually they have shafts of Tournai marble and onyx marble on them. On the south-west corner of the cloister it is possible to see part of the undercroft of Bishop Ernulf's cellarer's range, with next to it the lavatorium and doorway into the refectory, which were rebuilt in the early 13th century. In the early 14th century a bridge was built across the west end of the chapter house to allow the monks access to the choir, built about a century earlier. Inside the cathedral there is a superb early 14th-century doorway at the end of this passage; the monks' choir stalls, though restored, are the earliest surviving timber choir stalls in England. The choir and eastern arm of the cathedral were rebuilt and greatly enlarged after a major fire in 1179, and though the main transepts were also rebuilt in the mid 13th century, the rebuilding of the nave was never carried out. This left it with its fine mid 12th-century arcades

BELOW: *The cathedral and priory precinct from the top of the Norman keep. The cloister garth is behind the large trees on the south-east side of the cathedral, while the bishop's palace was in the foreground.*

and west front. Some other remains of the monastery can be seen around the cathedral, particularly the three gateways: the early 16th-century cemetery gate on the north (this was the main entry from the city), the sacristy gateway beside the old bell tower (now called 'Gundulf's Tower'), and the so-called 'Prior's Gate' on the south. Overshadowing the whole precinct is Rochester Castle, with its very tall early 12th-century keep, and its 14th-century curtain wall on the east. Twice, in 1215 and 1264, this castle was besieged, leaving the priory desecrated and pillaged. Much rebuilding followed, culminating in the building of the tower and spire in 1343 (rebuilt in 1904).

LEFT: *Façade of the early 12th-century chapter house and dormitory in the east cloister walk. The deanery (earlier the prior's house) is behind.*

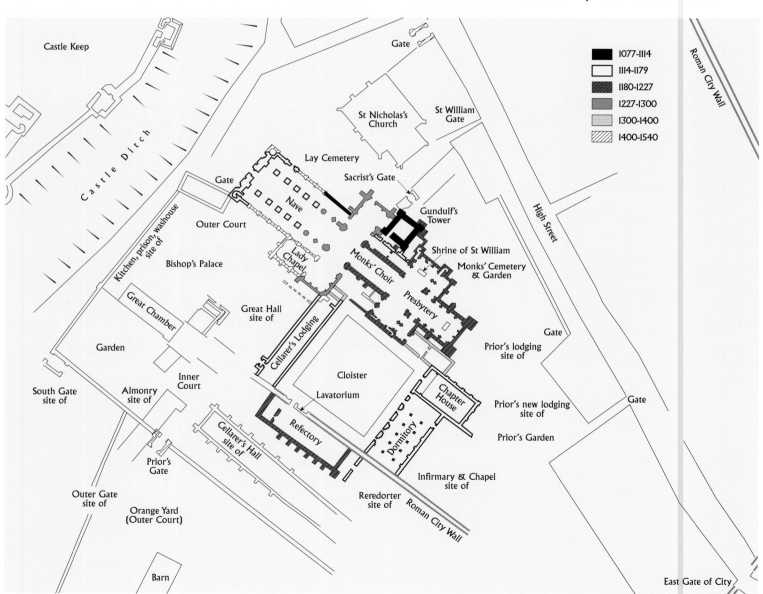

Castle Keep

Gate

Roman City Wall

1077-1114
1114-1179
1180-1227
1227-1300
1300-1400
1400-1540

St Nicholas's Church

St William Gate

Castle Ditch

Lay Cemetery

Sacrist's Gate

Gate

Gundulf's Tower

Nave

Shrine of St William

Kitchen, prison, washouse site of

Outer Court

Lady Chapel

Monks' Choir

Monks' Cemetery & Garden

High Street

Bishop's Palace

Cellarer's Lodging

Presbytery

Great Chamber

Great Hall site of

Gate

Garden

Prior's lodging site of

South Gate site of

Almonry site of

Inner Court

Cloister

Lavatorium

Chapter House

Prior's new lodging site of

Gate

Prior's Garden

Cellarer's Hall site of

Refectory

Dormitory

Prior's Gate

Infirmary & Chapel site of

Outer Gate site of

Reredorter site of

Roman City Wall

Orange Yard (Outer Court)

Barn

East Gate of City

Holy Trinity Priory

NORWICH, NORFOLK

ABOVE: *Christ seated in judgement on a large boss in the west cloister walk. Below him are kneeling monks and nuns.*

RIGHT: *The Ethelbert gate, with its restored 'flushwork' gable was built in 1316–17, after its predecessor had been destroyed in the 1272 riots.*

After the Norman Conquest, Herfast, the bishop of East Anglia (1070–84), was told by Archbishop Lanfranc to relocate his see from North Elham to Thetford, a more suitable urban site, and this was done in 1072. He had hoped to take over the great abbey at Bury St Edmunds as his see, but was prevented from doing so in 1081 by William the Conqueror, whose chaplain Herfast had been. Three years later he died and, in 1091, a Norman monk, Herbert of Losinga, became bishop. He had been prior of Fécamp Abbey and then abbot of Ramsey, and he is said to have paid William Rufus £1,900 for his appointment: a gross act of simony for which he later repented. At Thetford, Losinga replaced the secular canons at the cathedral with a community of Benedictine monks, but it is likely that there was already a plan in hand to move to the large city of Norwich, because Domesday Book records that Bishop Herfast had been given 14 houses there 'for the principal seat of the bishopric'. The formal move took place in 1094, and in the following year work started on a magnificent new cathedral and Benedictine priory.

By the time of Herbert's death in 1119, the whole of the eastern arm had been built, as well as the first four bays of the nave. This allowed the monks' choir (now holding 60 monks) to extend from under the crossing to the east end of the nave. By the time of Herbert's successor, Everard of Calne (1121–45), the great Benedictine churches in East Anglia – Bury, Norwich and Ely – were actively competing with each other, and Everard completed the very long nave. Norwich did not get a huge west front, but it did acquire a magnificent late Romanesque crossing tower, covered in decoration. A spire was

ABOVE: *The Carnery Chapel from the west front of the cathedral. To the left is the Erpingham gateway.*

added to this in the late 13th century, but was blown over on to the presbytery in a great storm in 1362. (The present spire was built in the 1480s.)

While the building of the nave was taking place, a large new monastery was being erected to the south, as well as the bishop's residence to the north. The monastery was constructed around a very large cloister (second in size within Britain only to the secular cloister in Salisbury), which seems to have had fine carved Romanesque arcades. The monastery was damaged in the town riots of 1272, and the cloister was rebuilt, with fine stone vaults, in many stages between 1297 and the early 15th century. In the east walk one can see the tripartite opening to the chapter house – a building that was unfortunately demolished in 1830. At the north end of the east walk is the wonderful early 14th-century doorway into the nave; at the west end of the north walk is the fine barrel-vaulted parlour. The west range, now in ruins, became the guest hall in the 13th century. The south range contained the huge monks' refectory (now the brand-new cathedral refectory), and the 12th-century north wall of this still stands to its full height. South of this building was the late 12th-century monastic infirmary; this, tragically, was demolished in 1804, but parts of five piers from the south arcade in the infirmary hall survive. East of this was the prior's house, now the deanery, which incorporates part of the east wall of the 12th-century great dormitory, and the north wall of the reredorter. To the west of these buildings was the outer court of the monastery, with two fine gatehouses on its west side. Opposite the west front of the cathedral is the main gate, the Erpingham Gate (built in 1416–35), while to the south-west is the St Ethelbert Gate (built in 1316–20). Its predecessor was badly damaged in the 1272 riots. To the east of the cathedral and monastery, the close extends over the old water meadows (now playing fields) to the 15th-century water gate on the River Wensum, beside Pull's Ferry.

St Etheldreda's Priory

ELY, CAMBRIDGESHIRE

ABOVE: *Mid-15th-century panel showing St Etheldreda's incorrupt body being translated to a new shrine.*

RIGHT: *View west inside the monastic barn (now the school dining hall), with its crown-post roof of c. 1375*

omesday Book records Ely as the second richest abbey in England after Glastonbury. The great abbey had not at this time (1086) acquired its bishop, but its early Norman rebuilding, on a grand scale, was taking place under Abbot Simeon (1081–93), the brother of Bishop Walkelin of Winchester. The very large aisled transepts and nave are similar to those at Winchester, and it was the great reforming bishop of Winchester, St Æthelwold, who had reconstructed the Anglo–Saxon church here in AD 970, after a large new body of Benedictine monks had been installed. The first monastery on this large island in the Fens had been founded 300 years earlier in AD 673 by St Etheldreda, a daughter of the king of the East Angles who had married the king of Northumbria. By the time of her death six years later she had established a successful 'double' monastery (for both monks and nuns) which flourished until destroyed by the Vikings in AD 870. In 1106, when the eastern arm of the large new Norman abbey church was complete, the remains of St Etheldreda were translated to a new shrine at the east end of the church. Work then continued on the long nave, and on the high western façade with its flanking apsidal chapels. During this period of renewed activity, the new diocese of Ely was

ABOVE: *The interior of the wonderful chapel built in the early 14th century by Prior Crauden for his house.*

ABOVE RIGHT: *One of the late 12th-century arcades in the infirmary hall, with later medieval chambers built into the aisle behind it.*

created from a small eastern section of the vast diocese of Lincoln. In October 1109, the pope having given his consent, Hervey, the bishop of Bangor, was enthroned as the first bishop of Ely. Ely then became a cathedral priory, with the bishop (the titular abbot), appointing the prior to run the monastery.

Sadly, most of the core buildings of Ely Priory, around a large cloister, have been destroyed: only a few fragments remain of the chapter house, dormitory and refectory. Beyond this to the east and south (and north of the cathedral), however, some of the other priory buildings are well preserved. To the south of the cloister are parts of the great kitchen and its neighbouring guest houses (now the bishop's residence), and beyond this is the prior's house, built for Prior Crauden in about 1325, with its exquisite first-floor chapel. Further south, several other monastic buildings survive, ending with the great gate of the priory (known as Ely Porta). Next to it was a great barn, and the remains of the motte and bailey castle (now Cherry Hill). Running down the hill to the north-east is the 'Dean's Meadow', formerly the monks' vineyard. To the east of the cloister, the large infirmary hall and chapel (with its own vaulted sanctuary) were built in the later 12th century. One can still see the remains of the fine late Romanesque arcades of both hall and chapel, because only the central space was unroofed after the Dissolution. In the side aisles a whole series of later chambers were created for the sub-prior, cellarer, infirmarer, etc., and these were retained and enlarged for the dean and chapter appointed in 1541 after the Dissolution. North-east of the cathedral is the monks' wonderful Lady chapel, and beyond this, on the high street frontage, is another gateway, and also the remains of the almonry and sacristan's houses. By the 15th century the bishop of Ely was a great figure in England. His principal residence sat immediately west of the cathedral, and though most of it has been destroyed, two great brick-built wings can still be seen.

NORMAN MONASTERIES
(Benedictines)

After the Norman Conquest, a number of new abbeys were built, including Battle Abbey. Several other great abbeys came into being in large towns such as Gloucester or Chester, where the local Norman earls were powerful patrons. Gloucester also had several royal connections, and acquired the tomb of the murdered King Edward II. At York, a very large new abbey was built outside the city walls on the west; after

the unrest of the late 13th century, it was given its own fortifications.

Many of the greater abbeys obtained new daughter houses after the Norman Conquest, sometimes far away from the mother house (as at Binham). Finchale was a daughter house of, and close to, Durham, but its origins were as a 12th-century hermitage. In the late middle ages, it became a fine holiday house for the monks of Durham.

ABOVE: *A cowled figure emerging from foliage on a boss at St Mary's Abbey, York.*

BELOW: *View of the ruins of Finchale priory church from across the River Wear.*

Battle Abbey

BATTLE, EAST SUSSEX

HISTORY

- *c.*1070 Founding of abbey
- 1094 Consecration of abbey by Archbishop Anselm
- 13th century – Most abbey buildings rebuilt, and large abbot's house created
- 1538 Abbey dissolved and estate acquired by Sir Anthony Browne

SPECIAL FEATURES

- Great gatehouse of 1338
- Great vaulted chambers below the dormitory
- Remains of crypt at east end of large abbey church
- Site of battlefield of Hastings

ABOVE: *The monks' common room, which probably contained braziers in the winter.*

RIGHT: *The magnificent 1338 gatehouse, which looks out on to the marketplace.*

OPPOSITE: *Late 13th-century arcading beside the abbot's house in the west cloister walk.*

O NE OF THE MOST FAMOUS DATES in English history is 14 October 1066: the day of the battle of Hastings, when William the Conqueror destroyed the Anglo–Saxon aristocracy of England along with its king, Harold Godwinson. This fine abbey was founded by King William a few years after the battle, in gratitude for his victory. The first monks came from the Benedictine abbey of Marmoutier on the river Loire, and the abbey church was deliberately laid out at the top of the hillside, where the fiercest fighting had taken place (the high altar was said to have been placed on the spot where Harold was killed).

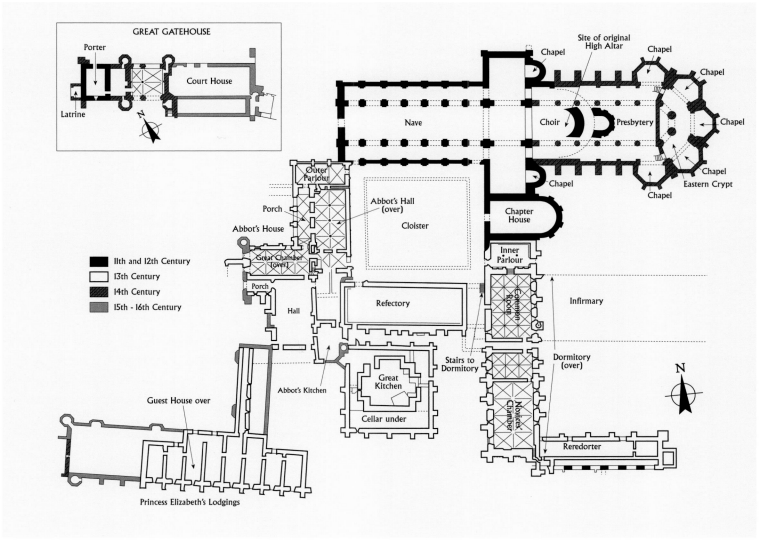

GREAT GATEHOUSE

Porter

Latrine

Court House

N

■ 11th and 12th Century
□ 13th Century
▨ 14th Century
▬ 15th - 16th Century

Site of original High Altar

Chapel

Chapel

Chapel

Chapel

Chapel

Eastern Crypt

Nave

Choir

Presbytery

Chapel

Chapel

Outer Parlour

Porch

Abbot's House

Abbot's Hall (over)

Cloister

Chapter House

Great Chamber (over)

Porch

Hall

Refectory

Inner Parlour

Common Room

Infirmary

Stairs to Dormitory

Dormitory (over)

Abbot's Kitchen

Great Kitchen

Novices' Chamber

Guest House over

Cellar under

Reredorter

N

Princess Elizabeth's Lodgings

ABOVE: *The large buttressed south wall of the dormitory range, with the ruins of the reredorter on the right.*

This made it a difficult site for a monastery, but with the king funding all of the costs, the eastern arm was begun in about 1070 and consecrated in 1076. The cloister and domestic buildings were then built down the hillside to the south-west, and full consecration by Archbishop Anselm took place in February 1094, in the presence of King William Rufus. Of the 11th-century church and apsidal chapter house to the south, only the foundations are now visible, but the impressive ruins of the great dormitory range, which run down the hillside to the south of the chapter house, and the shell of the reredorter can still be clearly seen. The great dormitory, at the first-floor level, is now open to the air, but beneath it are the splendid remains of a series of mid 13th-century vaulted chambers. Particularly impressive is the novices' chamber at the southern end, with its central capitals, columns and bases of Purbeck marble. During the 13th century almost all the monastic buildings were rebuilt, and a magnificent new abbot's house was created on the west side of the cloister. This fine building survives, but much altered, as it was turned into a great country house in the 18th and 19th centuries. After the First World War it became a school, though it was badly damaged in a fire in 1931. After this it was carefully restored by the architect Sir Harold Brakspear. He also laid out parts of the cloister.

When the Hundred Years' War with France broke out in the 1330s, the abbots of Battle became the main organizers of the south coast defences in East Sussex. In 1377 Abbot Hamo himself, with a band of troops, repulsed French raiders at Winchelsea, an exploit for which he became famous. By this time the abbey precinct had become a fortress in its own right, with a great crenellated wall all around it. Most splendid of all the survivals is the great gatehouse (rebuilt in 1338) that looks out over the market place of the town. This is one of the finest medieval monastic gatehouses in England.

The abbey was dissolved on 27 May 1538, and Abbot John Hammond and 18 monks left. The magnificent estate was given to Sir Anthony Browne, Henry VIII's friend and Master of the Horse. The abbot, however, was given a generous pension of £100 a year, and lived in a house on the other side of Battle High Street until his death in 1546.

St Peter's Abbey

GLOUCESTER, GLOUCESTERSHIRE

ABOVE: *The fan-vaulted lavatorium in the north cloister walk, opposite the refectory.*

RIGHT: *The south arcade and west doorway (right) are all that remain of the infirmary hall.*

The great abbey of St Peter at Gloucester was one of the most magnificent in the west of England, and in 1541 the church became one of Henry VIII's new cathedrals. Architecturally it is one of the finest churches in England, with an amazing new 14th-century structure built into the early Norman eastern arm. Here is the tomb-shrine of the brutally murdered king Edward II, with above it the largest medieval window in England. The church has many other fine features, including a superb 15th-century crossing tower and very large eastern Lady chapel; it is also lucky in retaining some wonderful features of its neighbouring monastery (unlike the nearby Tewkesbury Abbey).

Immediately to the north of the nave is perhaps the most beautiful vaulted cloister in England; adjoining this on the east is a very fine Norman chapter house and a fragment of the great dormitory. To the north of the cloister is only the shell of the monks' refectory, but next to it part of the infirmary (or 'little') cloister survives, with, to the north-east, the arcades of the infirmary hall. To the north again are the remains, along the abbey boundary wall, of the abbot's house, which after 1541 became the bishop's palace. South of the cathedral is 'College Green', which was the outer court of the abbey (on the west) and the lay people's cemetery (to the east). The main outer gate to the

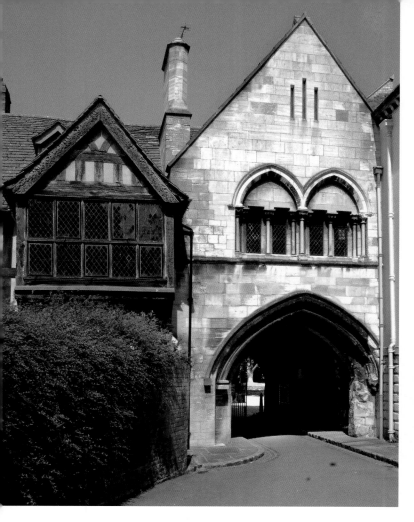

ABOVE: *View west through St Mary's Gate to the site of Bishop Hooper's martyrdom.*

ABOVE RIGHT: *The recesses in the north wall of the south cloister walk once contained the monks' carrels (writing desks).*

monastery, the 13th–century St Mary's Gate, still survives on the west side of College Green; just outside this gate Bishop John Hooper was burned at the stake in 1555. On the south–east is a 16th–century postern gate, made famous by Beatrix Potter's *The Tailor of Gloucester*, called St Michael's Gate.

A monastery was first created within the north–west corner of the Roman walled city of Gloucester in the late 7th century, but this was eclipsed by the nearby St Oswald's priory in the 10th century. However, King Alfred's daughter Ethelflaed was buried at St Peter's with her husband, Ethelred, and a reformed Benedictine monastery was created here in the early 11th century during the reign of King Cnut. A new church was begun in 1058, but it was only after the Norman Conquest that St Peter's became a major abbey. William the Conqueror built an important castle in the south–west corner of Gloucester, and in 1072 brought in his Norman chaplain, Serlo, as the new abbot. It was during the king's stay in Gloucester for Christmas 1085 that he commissioned the pro-duction of the Domesday Book. Four years after this, Abbot Serlo demolished the north–western city walls and started to put up a magnificent new Romanesque church. He started with the crypt, which can still be seen. By the time Serlo died in 1104, the abbey church was complete, and large new buildings were going up around the clois-ter for the 100 monks he had gathered around him. In the later 14th century this clois-ter was transformed into a miraculous space, with its beautiful early Perpendicular vaulting. It is here, more than anywhere else, that one can imagine the monks at work. In the south cloister walk are the recesses for the monks' carrels (writing desks), while in the north walk is the trough or lavatorium where the monks washed their hands before going into the refectory. There is even a cupboard recess for towels.

St Werburgh's Abbey

CHESTER, CHESHIRE

HISTORY

- Original church built in the early 10th century
- 1092 Work on new church and abbey buildings begins
- Later re-building at abbey
- 1540 Dissolution of abbey and creation of new cathedral

SPECIAL FEATURES

- Remains of 12th-century west range and abbot's house
- Fine 13th-century chapter house and vestibule, and refectory
- Early 16th-century cloisters with monks' carrels
- Abbey gateway

ABOVE: *The beautiful four-square vaulted vestibule to the chapter house, which can be glimpsed in the distance.*

RIGHT: *The abbey church (later the cathedral) from the south-west, with the large south transept (for the church of St Oswald) on the right.*

Like Gloucester Abbey, the Abbey of St Werburgh at Chester was built just inside the shell of a Roman walled city, and here too in 1541 the abbey church became a cathedral – in this instance for a new diocese covering the whole of north-west England. The abbey was established on its present site in 1092 by Hugh Lupus (i.e. 'Hugh the Wolf'), the second Norman earl of Chester, who was also the nephew of William the Conqueror. He was aided in this foundation by Anselm, the famous abbot of Bec in Normandy, who came to England and was not long afterwards made archbishop of Canterbury by King William Rufus. The first new monks at Chester were sent over from Bec Abbey, and soon afterwards work began on a large new abbey church. The lower walls of the north-west tower, north aisle and north transept from the earliest church all still survive, as does the undercroft of the cellarer's range on the west side of the cloister, where the cathedral shop is now. Between it and the north-west tower is a slightly later passage; above this is the mid 12th-century chapel of St Anselm (canonized in the 1160s), which was later attached to the neighbouring abbot's house (after 1541, the bishop's chapel).

The abbey church was extended in the early 13th century, but at the end of that century the whole eastern arm was rebuilt with a new shrine for St Werburgh and a Lady chapel. Also during the 13th century the principal monastic build-

ings on the north and east sides of the cloister were rebuilt. Off the east walk is still the very fine vaulted chapter house, which has its own square vestibule in front of it. This contains four piers which run straight into the vaults above, without intervening capitals. Next to it, on the north, is a contemporary vaulted passage that once led east to the infirmary. Beyond the passage is the vaulted undercroft, beneath the dormitory, which acted as the monks' warming house. In the cloister north walk, immediately to the east of the refectory door, is the monks' lavatorium. The refectory itself also survives; though it has been heavily restored, and now has a 20th-century roof, there remains in its south wall a magnificent late 13th-century reading pulpit, with a monumental stair leading up to it: one of the best of its kind to survive in Britain. The cloisters themselves were rebuilt very late, in the 1520s. They have also been heavily restored, but, as at Gloucester, the recesses for the monks' carrels can still be seen in the south and west walks. West of the cloisters was the outer court of the monastery (now Abbey Square), and on its south-west side is the 14th-century great gate to the abbey, leading out into the market place in Northgate Street. It has three bays of vaulting and a pedestrian gate as well as the principal one. On the north and east, the abbey precinct was surrounded and protected by the city walls (still, in part, Roman), but the monks were allowed to make a small postern gate, Kaleyard Gate, in the eastern city walls.

In the mid 14th century one of the monks of Chester, Ranulph Higden, wrote one of the largest and most illuminating of medieval monastic chronicles, the *Polychronicon*. He was summoned to Edward III's court at Westminster, and became the abbey's most famous monk.

BELOW: *The restored refectory, looking east, with the doorway to the pulpit (just visible above) in the south-east corner.*

St Mary's Abbey

YORK, YORKSHIRE

The huge abbey church of St Mary, 360 feet long, which lay in its own precinct just west of the walled city of York, was second only in size in York to the Minster. It stood at the centre of one of the most splendid Benedictine abbeys in the north of England, out-ranked only by Durham Cathedral Priory. A group of Benedictine monks, who had had to flee first from Whitby and then from Lastingham, were given the church of St Olave outside the west gate of York in 1086 by Alan, earl of Richmond. In 1088 their site was greatly enlarged by King William Rufus, and the following year work started on a great new Norman church east of St Olave's. The plan of this building (now partly marked out on the ground) is known from excavation: its eastern apsidal chapels are reminiscent of Archbishop Lanfranc's cathedral at Canterbury and St Alban's Abbey. Between 1271 and the beginning of the 14th century the abbey church was completely rebuilt, and the fine ruins that have survived to the present day are of this period. Particularly impressive are the eight-bayed north wall of the nave, in the English Geometrical style, and the remains of the west front. During the time when this work was being carried out, a large new nave was also being erected at the nearby Minster.

By the 14th century, the very powerful abbot of St Mary's was allowed to wear a

ABOVE: *The rebuilt, highly decorated late 12th-century entrance to the chapter house in the Yorkshire Museum.*

RIGHT: *The shell of the main 12th-century gatehouse that now acts as the entrance to the public gardens.*

ABOVE: *The north-west corner of the large late 13th-century nave of the abbey church.*

mitre (one of only a handful of 'mitred abbots' in the north of England), and he also sat in Parliament. He administered justice and collected taxes in his own 'Liberty of St Mary's' in Bootham outside the west gate of the city, and was very unpopular with the local people as a result. In 1262 the abbot had to flee after a riot in Bootham, and four years later a large stone wall was put up around the precinct. It was heightened in 1318 and given towers and battlements, and on the north and west these can still be seen. The principal abbey gatehouse is also still visible on the west side, beside the rebuilt St Olave's church. It dates in part from the late 12th century, but was rebuilt in the 13th. Early in the 14th century King Edward II used the abbey for his chancery when engaged in his Scottish wars, and by this time the precinct was well fortified.

Not much now survives above ground of the main monastic buildings around the cloister, but in the late 1820s the very fine late 12th-century vestibule to the chapter house was uncovered, along with the narrow passage against the south transept to the north of it. This, and the fireplace of the warming house to the west, can now be seen – still *in situ* – in the basement of the Yorkshire Museum, which was built over it. The museum also contains many other fine architectural fragments from the excavations.

Adjoining the monastic buildings on the north-east was the late medieval abbot's house, which was rebuilt in brick from 1483. After the Dissolution of the abbey in 1539, the abbot's house became the palace for the king's 'Council of the North', and was known (and is still known) as 'the King's Manor'. Much building work took place in the late 16th and early 17th centuries, continuing until the Council's abolition in 1641. After suffering extensive damage in the Civil Wars, the abbey precinct became a useful 'quarry' for building stone in the 18th century, providing stone for, among other things, the county gaol and Ouse Bridge.

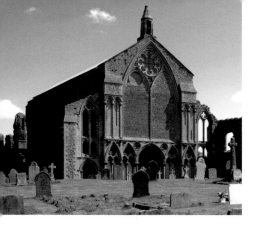

Binham Priory

BINHAM, NORFOLK

ABOVE: *The magnificent c.1240 west front of the church, with its early tracery.*

RIGHT: *The well-preserved early 12th-century three tiers of walling on the north side of the nave. All of the upper openings are now blocked.*

any of the biggest Benedictine abbeys had their own dependent cells at an early date, and Binham was one of eight such houses, each ruled by a prior, attached to the great abbey of St Alban's. Lying only 2½ miles inland from the north Norfolk coast on the north–west side of the once much more populous village of Binham, it was founded in about 1091 by Peter de Valognes, Lord of Orford, a nephew of William the Conqueror.

As in many Benedictine abbeys, the nave of the church was used as the local parish church, and this continued after the priory was dissolved in 1539, though sadly without its original side aisles (the north aisle was demolished only in 1809). At the east end of the church is a medieval stone screen with doors in it on either side of the altar. After the Dissolution the doors were blocked and the screen was built up right to the roof, with only a tall 'domestic' window in its east wall; many of the structures beyond it, such as the monks' choir and presbytery, were soon pulled down. Some very tall chunks of masonry were left, however, and with the removal of the rubble around them in 1934–8, one can now see much of the original form of the transepts and eastern arm of the priory church.

The first monastic church was built in the early 12th century with apsidal eastern chapels, as

ABOVE: *The remains of the massive Norman piers on the north side of the presbytery.*

RIGHT: *View north of the cellarer's range and the prior's house on the west side of the cloister.*

at St Alban's. Only the foundations of these survive, because in the later middle ages the sanctuary was enlarged and then given more substantial chapels on either side, including a Lady chapel on the north. There was a large crossing tower, and though this was demolished soon after 1539, some large sections of the early 12th-century crossing piers can still be seen. Only about two-thirds of the parochial nave was completed in the 12th century, and in 1212, with the reign of King John approaching its chaotic end, the priory was under siege from Robert Fitzwalter, one of the king's enemies. He was driven off by the king's forces; with the accession of the new king, Henry III, a much more prosperous period returned, and under Prior Richard du Parc (1227–44) the nave was at last completed and given a fine new west front. This exceptional piece of work, in the early French Gothic style, is now the glory of the abbey. It was finished in the early 1240s, before the very large-scale work, in the same style, at Westminster Abbey got under way in 1246.

In 1933 the area around the parish church was bought by the Norfolk Archaeological Trust, so that the ruins of the monastery itself could be uncovered. This was done between 1934 and 1938, and one is now able to walk through the south door in the west front to the outer parlour of the priory (above which was probably the prior's chapel). From here one enters the cloister, with the low walls around it of the principal buildings. On the east are the chapter house and the entrance to the day stairs to the dormitory. Below this was the warming house (with fireplace) in the dormitory undercroft. On the south side of the cloister was the refectory; the base of the reading pulpit can be seen on the south-east. Beyond is the shell of the monks' kitchen. The west range was the cellarer's range; above it was probably the prior's house. Most of the ruins are of flint-rubble masonry, but some fine carved Barnack stone, for the dressings, can also be seen. Around the whole site was a stone wall, parts of which survive, and on the west the remains of the principal gatehouse are visible at the site entrance.

Finchale Priory

COUNTY DURHAM

HISTORY

- 1110 Godric settles at Finchale.
- 1170 Death of Godric
- 1237 Work on church and priory buildings begins
- c.1364 Adaptation of domestic buildings as monks' holiday house
- Early 15th century – prior's house converted
- 1538 Dissolution of priory

SPECIAL FEATURES

- St Godric's chapel and tomb
- Shell of mid 13th–century church, with blocked arcades
- Ruins of claustral buildings
- Prior's house

ABOVE: *View north-west down the church, showing the arcades that were blocked in 1364-5, and given new windows.*

RIGHT: *View south-east across the cloister garth to the chapter house and refectory (right).*

his is one of the most interesting, and unusual, monastic sites in England. It is beautifully situated in a bend in the river Wear, 4 miles downstream from, and north–east of, Durham. It started life as the site for a hermitage of an extraordinary man called Godric. Born in Walpole, Norfolk, he became a sea–captain and pirate; then, having been caught up in the First Crusade, in 1101 he made the pilgrimage to Jerusalem, returning via Compostela. He also made pilgrimages to Rome (once accompanied by his elderly mother). In about 1105 he sold all his goods and tried to become a hermit in northern England. After various attempts in different places, he made another penitential pilgrimage to Jerusalem, where he visited the holy places and lived for a time in the desert with hermits. After returning to England and resuming his travels around the country, he was finally allowed to settle on the bishop of Durham's land at Finchale in 1110. Amazingly, he lived on for another 60 years, dying on 12 May 1170 aged over 100. At Finchale a stone chapel of St John the Baptist was built for him, and after his death this was taken over by the monks of Durham, two of whom lived here until 1195. At that point Bishop Hugh de Puiset gave it to the Augustinian canons, but it was soon returned to the

ABOVE: *View north-east across the ruins of the prior's chamber, which in the late middle ages became the centre of the complex.*

monks of Durham, and became a separate priory, dependent on Durham Cathedral priory.

The present buildings were started in 1237, and a large aisled nave, transepts and an aisled chancel were put up on the site of St Godric's chapel. A cloister was also built, with a chapter house and dormitory on the east side and a refectory to the south. The principal walls of these buildings now form the 'skeleton' of the ruins on the site. By the early 14th century up to 15 monks were living here, with a prior in a separate house to the east of the cloister.

After the Black Death, and the havoc it wrought among the Durham monks, a new role was found for the priory. In about 1364–5 the aisles in the church were pulled down and the arcades were blocked up and replaced with windows. The domestic buildings of the priory were then adapted to serve as the Durham monks' holiday house. By the early 15th century the system was regulated, with a full-time prior and a 'staff' of four monks at Finchale; these would act as hosts to the monks – four at a time – who would come out from Durham for a three-week stay. The prior's house, which became the centre of this new regime, was rebuilt; only a ruined shell survives today, but one can still see how the two-storeyed lodging acquired a new large kitchen on the west. All the monks must have eaten at the prior's table in the first-floor hall. To the east of this was the prior's chamber, with its fine east window, and to the north was his private study, with an oriel window. South of the main chamber was the prior's chapel, with its own east window. In this splendid complex of buildings, in its beautiful rural setting, the late medieval monks of Durham sojourned in some style – until it was all swept away at the dissolution of Durham Cathedral Priory in 1538.

BLACK CANONS
(Augustinians)

The Canons regular (i.e. priests living by a rule) of St Augustine were a body of priests who following the ideas of St Augustine (bishop of Hippo, in modern Algeria, 392–430), and wore a black habit. Their Rule was not as strict as that of St Benedict, and many older non–monastic churches, such as St Frideswide's, became Augustinian houses in the early 12th century. At this time the archbishop of Canterbury,

William de Corbeil (1123–36) was an Augustinian, and the Augustinian priory at Carlisle was made a cathedral.

Later in the 12th century other important churches like Waltham were taken over by the Augustinians. Many of them had large parish churches within them, that continued after the Dissolution. Laycock Abbey, not founded until 1232, was unusual as a house for aristocratic ladies.

ABOVE: *A finely carved corbelled head in the chapter house at St Frideswide's Priory, Oxford.*

BELOW: *The view north-eastwards across the ruined cloister to Bolton abbey church. The nave is still the parish church.*

Waltham Abbey

WALTHAM, HERTFORDSHIRE

HISTORY

- *c.*1060 Church built by Harold Godwinson
- 1080s Church rebuilt
- 1177 Becomes an Augustinian Priory
- 1540 Dissolution of the abbey
- 1550 Demolition of building and building of west tower

SPECIAL FEATURES

- Early Norman work in east wall of present church
- Remains of large late 12th-century Augustinian church and cloister
- Late 14th-century gatehouse and bridge

ABOVE: *The late 14th-century gatehouse façade to the north of the abbey church.*

RIGHT: *The supposed site of the grave of King Harold in the presbytery of the Norman church. In the background is the east wall of the surviving parish church.*

n 1184 the church of the Holy Cross at Waltham, some 15 miles north of London in the Lee valley (now close to the noisy M25), was made into a 'mitred abbey'. This was an abbey of high status where the abbot, like a bishop, wore a mitre; later he also had a seat in the House of Lords. In 1177 the community of secular canons here was replaced by Augustinian canons, and a very large new church was built with a cloister and large-scale monastic buildings to the north of it. That great new late 12th-century church has now been completely destroyed, though its foundations were partly uncovered in 1938–9, but in 1540 it was briefly listed as one of Henry VIII's new cathedrals (like Bury St Edmunds). In the event this transformation did not happen, and only the nave of the earlier western church was retained for the parish church.

The Anglo–Saxon origins of the church at Waltham are unknown, but a myth was later created about a cracked marble slab showing the crucifixion of Christ, which was brought to Waltham in the early 11th century. (Hence the dedication to the Holy Cross.) By the late 1050s the church had been given by King Edward the Confessor to Harold Godwinson – the king's brother-in-law, and famously (and briefly) king of England himself in 1066, before being killed at the Battle of Hastings. Just before this Harold had

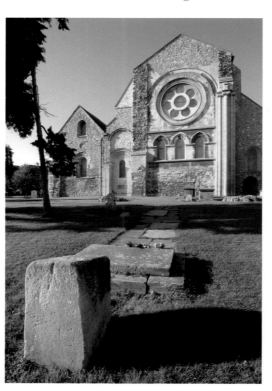

rebuilt the church at Waltham, and it was here that he wished to be buried; sadly, it is not known for certain if his body was ever interred here. It is more likely to have remained among the other war dead of October 1066 on the battleground beneath Battle Abbey. Harold's church at Waltham was replaced by a Norman church, the eastern arm of which, with its large apsidal ambulatory, was probably built in the 1080s. All that is visible today of this church is the west wall of the south transept (now visible as the southern part of the east wall of the surviving church). The nave of the Norman church was built in the early 12th century, and it is this very fine structure that is still visible in the parish church. The massive round piers are reminiscent of Durham Cathedral, with their deeply grooved spiral and chevron decoration. Above them are

ABOVE: *The impressive early 12th-century nave (now the parish church), with its Victorian ceiling and infilled east wall.*

typical Norman galleries and clerestories. The west end of the nave was partially rebuilt at the end of the 13th century and given a fine new west front. Unfortunately, this work was all mutilated in 1556, when a new west tower, made of reused materials, was stuck up against it after the earlier abbey towers had been demolished.

Today, traces of the Augustinian abbey buildings can be seen in the garden to the north and east of the present church. Most impressive are the 13th-century vaulted passage at the west end of the refectory, and the late 14th-century gatehouse and medieval bridge to the north of the west front of the church. Also dating from the 14th century is the chapel (now a Lady chapel) on the south side of the nave. On its east wall is a fine late 15th-century Doom painting which was rediscovered behind whitewash and plaster in 1876.

Lanercost Priory

LANERCOST, CUMBRIA

Some of the more important Augustinian priories were centred on large parish churches, and in these cases it was quite common for the parish church to survive in the nave after the Dissolution. This was what happened at Lanercost, where there is still a fine and flourishing parish church in the single–aisled nave, while the transepts, presbytery and sanctuary survive as a magnificent, largely intact but unroofed structure. The canons' main buildings around the cloister on the south have been demolished, except for the refectory under–croft and the west range which was converted into a house for Sir Thomas Dacre after the Dissolution. At its southern end is a partly ruined 'pele tower' (fortified residence) that was built for the Dacres. This reminds us that from the very end of the 13th century until 1603 Lanercost was close to England's northern border, and constantly in danger of being attacked by the Scots. West of the west range is another similar tower, the 'vicar's pele', against which the later vicarage was built.

The priory of St Mary Magdalene at Lanercost was founded in slightly more peaceful times, in about 1169 by Robert de Vaux. It lies less than a mile south of Hadrian's Wall in the beautiful valley of the Irthing. Only 11 miles to the west is Carlisle, where the cathedral, uniquely, was within another house of Augustinian canons (founded as a priory in 1122, it became a cathedral in 1133). At the end of the 13th century Lanercost

ABOVE: *The remains of the lavatorium in the north wall of the refectory undercroft.*

OPPOSITE: *View north-east across the early 13th-century presbytery. The canons' stalls were behind the large compound pier in the foreground.*

RIGHT: *View north-west across the remains of the cloister to the church. The chapter house was in the foreground on the right.*

ABOVE: *View east down the vaulted undercroft of the mid 13th-century refectory.*

found itself on the 'front line' during King Edward I's wars with Scotland, and was raided on several occasions. One such attack, in 1296, resulted in the burning of the cloister; but most ruinous of all was the six-month use of Lanercost made by King Edward and Queen Margaret in the winter of 1306–7. The 67-year old king was very ill, and special arrangements had to be made for him and his court at this time. Until new excavations are carried out we will not know where the king and queen lived, but it is likely that their lodgings were in the vicinity of the later vicarage, and that they were surrounded by a mass of timber buildings for all the 200 or so other members of the court. Eventually, in early 1307, the king left for a Parliament at Carlisle. He died only four months later, on 7 July, at Burgh by Sands on the Solway Firth.

The fine new church in which the king and queen and their court worshipped on the great festivals in 1306–7 still survives. It was built in stages between the later 12th and mid 13th centuries. The earliest masonry that can be seen is the lower south walls of the nave and the south transept. At the end of the 12th century the design of the presbytery and sanctuary was altered, and a magnificent three-storeyed elevation was erected. The nave was given a north aisle, and work on the west front was completed with a grand moulded west portal. In the gable above it there is still a fine contemporary statue of St Mary Magdelene, a rare survival.

The priory was suppressed in March 1537 for Henry VIII by the duke of Norfolk, but not finally dissolved until 8 January 1538, by which time the cloister and refectory had already been unroofed. The unroofing of the church followed, and for a time only the north aisle was used for the parish church. Later, in 1740–7, the nave was re-roofed and walled off from the shell of the eastern arm. This church was finally restored in the 1870s, but the eastern arm was left as a ruin (perhaps one day it too should be re-roofed!), within which are the decaying monumental early Tudor tombs of the Dacre family.

St Frideswide's Priory

OXFORD, OXFORDSHIRE

HISTORY

- *c.*AD 900 Creation of first church
- *c.*1120 Becomes an Augustinian priory
- *c.*1160–1200 Building of present church
- 1524 Dissolution of priory by Cardinal Wolsey.

SPECIAL FEATURES

- Mid 12th-century chapter house entrance
- Late 12th-century Canons' church (now cathedral)
- Remains of chapter house and dormitory
- Newly restored shrine of St Frideswide

church dedicated to St Frideswide, a semi–mythical saint of the late 7th to early 8th century, was probably created in the extreme south–east corner of the fortified Anglo–Saxon town of Oxford in about AD 900. This first church was burnt by the Danes in 1002, but was restored by King Edward the Confessor in 1049, and then looked after by a body of secular canons. By the early 12th century it was a free royal chapel, and Henry I turned it into a new house for Augustinian canons, at the suggestion of his justiciar Roger, bishop of Salisbury. The new canons were installed in about 1120, under a royal chaplain, Master Wimund, who acquired a group of regular canons from the important Augustinian house at Holy Trinity Priory, Aldgate, in London.

Some time after about 1140 work started on a new set of communal buildings

ABOVE: *High above the windows at the west end of the chapter house can be seen these 13th-century grotesques.*

RIGHT: *The newly reconstructed 1289 shrine of St Frideswide in the south-eastern part of the Latin chapel.*

ABOVE: *Late 14th-century figure of St Frideswide in the stained glass of the Latin chapel.*

ABOVE RIGHT: *The remaining east cloister walk with the magnificent 12th-century doorway into the chapter house on the right.*

around a cloister, and fragments of these still survive, including the west façade of the chapter house, a vaulted through-passage to the north of it, and fragments of the dormitory on the south-east. The work was carried out under the prior, Robert of Cricklade, who also started to build a new church with double aisles in both the nave and eastern arm. At the end of the 12th century there were 18 canons, and a grand new aisled north transept was being built with a special double eastern chapel for a new shrine of St Frideswide. The saint's relics were translated to this new shrine in 1180, and it became a popular place of pilgrimage, especially for women. A new Lady chapel was added to the east of the shrine in about 1230, and this was enlarged when a further new shrine was created in 1289. This shrine survived until 1538, and was reconstructed at the east end of the Lady chapel in 1889–91. It has just been restored again. The most prominent survival at St Frideswide's today, however, is the fine early 13th-century tower and stone spire over the crossing. At this time, also, the chapter house was rebuilt and given fine quadripartite rib vaults, with bosses showing the Virgin, Christ seated, St Frideswide, and four lions with one head. In the 14th century the Lady chapel acquired an outer aisle (the so-called 'Latin chapel'), which covered the shrine, and in the 15th century the main nave was re-roofed, followed by the eastern arm. The new early 15th-century nave roof was only of timber, but the presbytery was given a wonderful stone pendant-vault beneath its roof in about 1500.

As is well known, St Frideswide's priory was suppressed by Cardinal Wolsey in 1524 so that he could make his own very grand Cardinal's College here. The west end of the church and the west cloister range were very quickly demolished to make way for the vast outer court of the new college, but Wolsey's fall from grace in 1529 stopped all other work in its tracks, and only because of this have the rest of the church, and canons' buildings around the cloister, survived. Henry VIII did keep the new college here, now called Christ Church, but he reused the old church as the college chapel. Rather remarkably, this chapel became Oxford Cathedral as well in 1546, and as such it survives to this day.

Lacock Abbey

LACOCK, WILTSHIRE

ABOVE: *A mermaid on one of the 15th-century cloister vault bosses.*

RIGHT: *Part of the north walk of the very fine 15th-century lierne-vaulted cloister.*

 acock Abbey, in north–west Wiltshire, is perhaps most famous now as a fine National Trust house and the place where William Henry Fox Talbot took the first photograph in England in 1835. It lies to the east of a small town (much used as a film set), and between 1232 and 1539 was a nunnery for Augustinian canoness- es. At first sight, the house now appears to be no more than an 18th–century 'Gothick' mansion, but inside, at ground–floor level, much of the mid 13th-century vaulted undercrofts of the nuns' domestic buildings still survives around a beautiful cloister. Only the church, which was on the south, was completely removed soon after 1539. Its foundations, however, were uncovered in 1898 by Sir Harold Brakspear, and this showed that the nave and chancel were built as one con- tinuous rectangular structure, without transepts, and about 150 feet long. In the early 14th century quite a large Lady chapel was added on the south- east. Much of the north wall of the church sur- vives as the south front of the house, with a fine octagonal tower at its east end. This tower was built in the later 1540s, immediately after the church had been oblit- erated.

The abbey was founded by Ela, countess of Salisbury, who had been married to William Longespee, the illegitimate son of King Henry II and

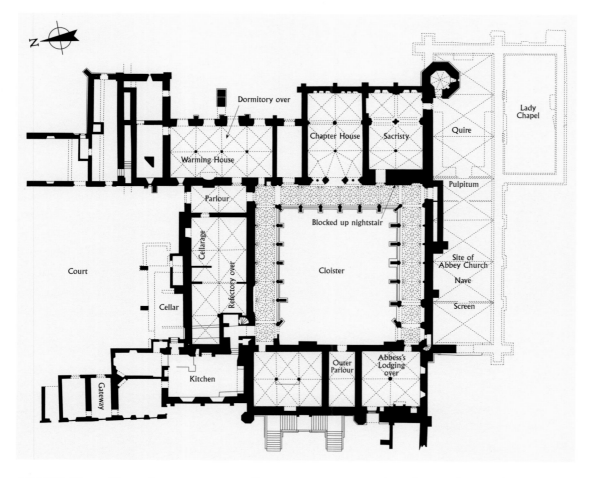

ABOVE: *Plan of Laycock Abbey based on that made by the architect, Sir Harold Brakspear. He excavated the foundations of the church (on the right) in 1898.*

half-brother to King John. They had both been closely involved with the start of work on building the new Salisbury Cathedral in 1220. After Longespee's death in 1226, Ela founded two religious houses in his memory: one, for men, was the Charterhouse at Hinton in Somerset; the other was this very aristocratic Augustinian abbey for women. Both were officially started on the same day, 16 April 1232, and the countess is said to have ridden the 16 miles between the two places in one day to be present at both ceremonies. The main buildings were rapidly erected over the next few years, using high-quality Haslebury stone from a quarry near Box, five miles to the west, and in 1238 Ela herself became a member of the community. In 1241, by which time it is likely that the main buildings were complete, she officially became the first abbess. Ela lived on for another 20 years, and on her death in 1261 was buried in the nuns' choir, a greatly respected founder who had gained many rights for the abbey. The family connection continued after her death, as her youngest son, Nicholas, became canon treasurer at Salisbury Cathedral and rector of Lacock. He became bishop of Salisbury in 1291; after his death in 1297, his heart was buried at Lacock. The abbey continued to flourish during the later medieval period with between 15 and 25 nuns, all from rich families. The more relaxed discipline of an Augustinian house suited them well.

At the core of the present house is the beautiful 15th-century lierne-vaulted cloister, with the original chapter house off the centre of the east walk. There is a central doorway flanked by double windows with Y-tracery, and inside a mass of beautiful moulded arches. Next to it on the south is a large sacristy, also covered with quadripartite rib vaulting and nearly as big in area as the chapter house. Within its east wall is the night stair, which connected the nuns' choir on the south with the dormitory that was above the whole west range. North of the chapter house is a through passage and a warming house, also covered by rib vaults and containing a large fireplace. Beyond is the sub-vault to the reredorter (latrine). Similar quadripartite rib-vaulted rooms can be seen in the north and west ranges, and above these were the refectory and abbess's house. Right from the beginning Abbess Ela's house in the west range must have been a very grand affair, but all the principal rooms were transformed in the mid 18th century into a 'Gothick' hall and dining room for the Talbot family.

ABOVE: *A fine cedar tree obscures the Tudor south front and tower – the latter was built in the 1540s, soon after the demolition of the abbey church.*

RIGHT: *The warming house below the dormitory in the east range (note the contemporary fireplace). The cauldron, made of bell metal, has an inscription on it recording its manufacture in 1500.*

Bridlington Priory

BRIDLINGTON, YORKSHIRE

ABOVE: *Late medieval corbel in the abbey gatehouse of a man playing the bagpipes.*

RIGHT: *Reconstructed section of the very fine mid 12th-century cloister arcade.*

hat remains of one of the largest and richest Augustinian houses in England now lies in the 'Old Town' just south–west of Flamborough Head, overlooking Bridlington Bay. The priory was founded in 1113–14 by Walter, son of Gilbert de Gant, one of the new Norman aristocrats in northern England. His grave in the original church was probably marked by the wonderful early 12th-century slab of black Tournai marble that is still preserved in the present church, adorned with some splendidly carved early Romanesque beasts, and a very crude representation of the church. Over the course of the 12th century Walter de Gant's priory created a market town at Bridlington and established jurisdiction over the profitable seaport, and became very wealthy as a result.

During the 13th century a very large church was built, about 333 feet long. The nave was the town's parish church, and sadly it is only this part of the building that stands today – still as the parish church. Even so, the grandeur of the surviving structure, with

its two western towers, still shows us what a magnificent church it once was. Most of what we see now dates from the 13th century, but the south–west tower, and the fine west doorway with a very large west window above, were rebuilt in the 15th century. The upper parts of both towers were designed by George Gilbert Scott, and built in the 1870s.

Bridlington priory continued to flourish in the later middle ages, gaining a reputation as a centre of learning: several of its canons were literary scholars and 'scientists', such as George Ripley, a 15th-century canon, who was a very well-known philosopher and alchemist). Its most famous canon, however, was John of Thwing, who went to Oxford University and on his return to Bridlington was made precentor and then cellarer. From 1362 until his death in 1379 he served as the prior, with a great reputation for holiness. After his death, miracles were reported at his tomb, and in 1401 he was canonized by Pope Boniface IX. A magnificent new shrine was created at the east end of the church, and his remains were translated there on 11 March 1404 by Archbishop Richard Scrope of York. When Henry V won the battle of Agincourt in 1415, he attributed his success to the intercession of his two Yorkshire saints, John of Beverley and John of Bridlington. All of this greatly enhanced the priory's status, and in 1409 the prior became a 'mitred' prior – a distinction shared in Yorkshire only by the two

BELOW: *View of the church from the south-east, showing the north wall of the former cloister. The buttressing beyond it was put up after the prior's house was demolished.*

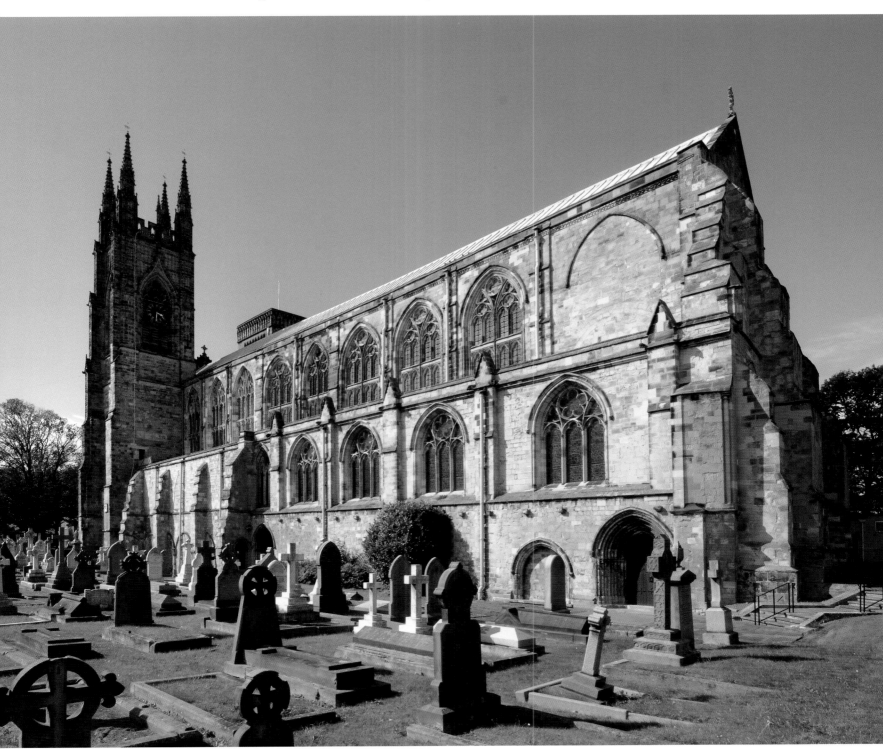

Benedictine abbots at Selby and St Mary's, York.

Sadly, virtually nothing now survives of the priory above ground, as the eastern arm and all the monastic buildings were demolished soon after the Dissolution in 1539. The last prior, William Wode, was involved in the clerical protest against Henry VIII's reforms, the 'Pilgrimage of Grace', and was hanged at Tyburn in London in 1537. At the same time the 26 other canons were expelled.

The original main entry to the church was through the fine 13th-century porch and doorway on the north side of the nave. Outside the much narrower south aisle one can still see traces of the north cloister walk, and the two doorways going into it, on the east. To the west are traces of the north wall of the vaulted undercroft that was once part of the prior's home. Inside the present church (at the west end of the north aisle) one can also see two reconstructed fragments of the very fine mid 12th-century cloister arcades. Otherwise, all that now survives of the priory buildings is the large late 14th-century gatehouse on the south-west, now called 'The Bayle'.

BELOW: The large 14th-century gatehouse to the priory, called 'The Bayle' – seen from the north-west.

Norton Priory

RUNCORN, CHESHIRE

ABOVE: *Detail of superbly carved corbel head on the cloister arcade.*

RIGHT: *The fine later 12th-century ribbed-vaults and piers in the undercroft of the west range, which were retained in the basement of the post-Dissolution country houses on the site.*

his priory is the only Augustinian house to have been archaeologically excavated in modern times. As a result of this, its architectural development is better understood than that of any other, despite the fact that only the vaulted undercroft of the later 12th-century west range survived above ground. Between 1971 and 1982 the whole of the church and all the buildings around the cloister were carefully excavated, and these are now displayed in an excellent parkland site, with a fine new museum in it, setting out all the finds and telling the story of the priory and the later country houses that succeeded it. All this was able to happen because the Norton Priory site lay within the new town development of Runcorn on the south side of the Mersey.

The priory was founded in about 1115, and was originally built in Runcorn itself. Then, in 1134, it was moved to Norton, 2½ miles to the east. The site chosen was on slightly elevated ground a mile south of the river Mersey, and not far from Halton Castle, the home of the original founders. The excavations revealed that a temporary church and a group of timber-framed buildings were quickly put up for the canons to

use while the first stone buildings were being erected. These were fairly modest in size, with an unaisled nave, transepts flanking the canons' choir and a small sanctuary. To the south of the church was a small cloister surrounded by the usual buildings: sacristy, chapter house, dormitory, refectory and cellarer's range. These were probably complete by the 1160s, but almost immediately the south and west ranges were demolished and replaced by a larger cloister, refectory and cellarer's range – whose quadripartite rib-vaulted undercroft still survives. Just after this the nave of the church was extended westward; then work started on a substantial enlargement of the eastern arm, continuing in several stages during the 13th century. A much larger chapter house was also built.

All of this expansion was a result of the house's increasing wealth through endowments, and the consequent increase in the number of canons, 26 of whom now occupied a dormitory that had been extended southwards and given an enlarged reredorter (latrine). The eastern chapels were becoming more elaborate at this time, again as shown by the recent excavations; and on the north-east was a large Lady chapel that was used for burials by the Dutton family, who in

ABOVE: *The magnificent late 12th-century doorway into the west range undercroft which was preserved in the 1868 west porch (hence Victorian tiles in foreground) of the Georgian country house.*

the later medieval period were the principal benefactors of the priory. Among many other important discoveries was the 13th-century bell-casting pit, with substantial traces of the mould for a bell. A replica bell now hangs in the site. In the late medieval period the number of canons declined, and the remaining domestic buildings were rebuilt to make them into much more comfortable accommodation for those who remained. The excavations were also able to show how a very elaborate enclosed cloister was built not long before the Dissolution.

In 1391 the prior was made an abbot and entitled to wear a mitre. This increased status is reflected in the abbot's house in the west range, which was rebuilt with a large tower block on its west side. This fine building survived the Dissolution in 1536 and was used by the Brooke family, who had acquired the site, until it was demolished in 1740. Luckily an engraving of the abbot's house was made just before its destruction.

Bolton Priory

NEAR SKIPTON, NORTH YORKSHIRE

HISTORY

- 1120 Foundation of Priory at Embsay
- 1151 Priory moved to Bolton
- Late 12th–early 14th centuries – much building work
- 1318–19 Wharfedale plundered by Scottish army

SPECIAL FEATURES

- Ruined shell of early 14th-century eastern arm
- Ruins of priory buildings around cloister to south
- 13th-century nave (now parish church)
- Uncompleted western tower of 1520

ABOVE: *View south-west from the south transept doorway across the ruined cloisters.*

RIGHT: *View south-eastwards to the river Wharfe, from near the foundations of the chapter house.*

he Priory of St Mary and St Cuthbert was originally founded in 1120 at Embsay, near Skipton, by William Meschines and his wife Cecily Rumeli, the lord of Skipton. Their daughter Alice Rumeli allowed the priory to be moved to Bolton in about 1151. The new site, beside the River Wharfe, lies in the south-east corner of the Yorkshire Dales National Park, and is one of the most beautiful enjoyed by any monastery.

As at Waltham, Lanercost and Bridlington, the nave of the priory church has survived as a parish church, and this is, of course, still roofed. To the east of it is the amazing shell of the completely rebuilt early 14th-century eastern arm, still retaining at its core the much smaller later 12th-century crossing and sanctuary. At the beginning of the 14th century the priory was very prosperous. There were about 15 canons, and the nave had been splendidly rebuilt and given a north aisle. Then in 1315–16 the harvests failed, and this disaster was followed in 1318–19 by the arrival of the Scottish army, who plundered all the priory's lands in Wharfedale. We are told that by the autumn of 1320 the community had been dispersed, as there were insufficient resources to maintain it.

ABOVE: *Doorway from the north-east corner of the cloister to the south transept. In the distance is the presbytery with its lower walls dating from the mid 12th-century.*

Nevertheless, it was soon re–established, and in the late 1320s the remarkable prior John of Laund started his great rebuilding work. Many parts of the walls of the new eastern arm still stand to their full height, but sadly most of the elaborate Decorated–style tracery in the very large window openings has disappeared. After the eastern arm was completed, the prior went on to rebuild the dormitory, and to create a complete–ly new house for himself immediately to the south of it. Even more remarkable was the building of a new octagonal chapter house to the east of the dormitory. This followed the great octagonal chapter house at York Minster in having no central pillar to sup–

ABOVE: *View of the shell of the wonderful new eastern arm of c.1330, seen from the modern churchyard on the south-east.*

port its roof. Only the lowest walls now survive of the domestic buildings around the cloister, as these were demolished soon after the Dissolution on 29 January 1540. South-west of these ruins part of the infirmary has survived, having been converted into a school and later incorporated into an enlarged rectory.

The one other survival at Bolton Priory is the lowest stage of a large new west tower, begun in 1520, as the inscription on it tells us. The magnificent structure was no doubt meant to rival Abbot Huby's great tower at Fountains Abbey, which is not far away across the moors to the north-east. The decoration on the tower is very ornate, but the money must have run out, for the work was left unfinished and remained so at the Dissolution. As a result, the original 13th–century west front of the church survives alongside the tower; had the tower been finished, the old west front would have been demolished to join the nave to the new tower arch. One wonders if Prior Richard Mone, the last prior, was intending to make his tower a very tall structure, like that at Fountains.

In the 19th century Bolton Priory, in its breathtaking setting, was written about and depicted by Romantic artists like Ruskin and Turner, and acquired the incorrect name of 'Bolton Abbey'. The main early 14th–century gatehouse to the west of the church was acquired by the Cavendish family (later the dukes of Devonshire), and given new wings to turn it into Bolton Hall.

BELOW: *General view of the Priory ruins from across the river Wharfe, to the south-east.*

BLACK MONKS
(Cluniacs)

The great abbey at Cluny in Burgundy had been founded in 910, and in the late 11th century, it was at the height of its power under its great abbot Hugh (1049–1109). When he died there were about 2,000 dependent monasteries in Europe. Of the dozen or so early foundations in England, Lewes, Castle Acre, Thetford and Wenlock were some of the most influential. They kept very close ties with the mother

house until the Hundred Years' War led to their being 'cut loose'. Reading, though founded from Cluny, quickly became independent as Henry I's private royal abbey. Henry of Blois, his nephew, was a Cluniac monk before becoming abbot of Glastonbury in 1126, and then bishop of Winchester. Henry's half–brother, King Stephen, founded his own Cluniac abbey mausoleum at Faversham in 1154.

ABOVE: *The prior's chapel (with its late 13th-century east window) in the prior's house at Castle Acre.*

BOTTOM: *The remains of Castle Acre priory church. The banded masonry in the foreground is from the late 11th-century church.*

Lewes Priory

LEWES, SUSSEX

HISTORY

- *c.*1081 Foundation of priory
- 1085 Burial of Gundrada at priory
- Mid 12th century – monks' dormitory and reredorter enlarged
- Late 12th–13th centuries – priory church enlarged
- 1537 Dissolution of priory

SPECIAL FEATURES

- Gundrada's graveslab in St John's church, Southover
- Remains of late 11th- and 12th-century reredorters
- Ruins of refectory and infirmary chapel
- Rebuilt gatehouse archway in 'Priory Crescent'

ABOVE: *Internal bases at the base of the south-west tower of the Norman priory church.*

RIGHT: *The Norman spiral staircase at the south-west corner of the ruins of the refectory building.*

The medieval walled town of Lewes is dominated by its castle, founded in the late 11th century by William de Warenne, who had been given the important late Anglo–Saxon borough there by William the Conqueror. Lewes lies on the tidal river Ouse, in East Sussex, a few miles inland from the sea. Immediately south of the town, at a place called Southover on the flatter land beside the river estuary, de Warenne and his wife Gundrada founded the Priory of St Pancras. To populate it they brought monks from the great abbey of Cluny in Burgundy, then at the height of its power: the pope himself, Gregory VII (1073–85), later canonized as St Hildebrand, was himself a former Cluniac, and his consent as well as that of King William had to be gained before monks from Cluny were allowed to come here to start the first new Cluniac priory in Britain, at Lewes.

Work on the great church got under way very quickly, and it was probably finished by 1085, when Gundrada was buried in it. Her husband, who towards the end of his life was made the earl of Surrey, was also buried there three years later, and by the mid 12th century the church had been enlarged to a huge size (about 430 feet long). Tragically, this magnificent building was systematically destroyed at the Dissolution, and then in 1845 a new railway line sliced right through the ruins of the cloister, chapter house and eastern arm of the great church. Amazingly, however, the lead coffins of de Warenne and Gundrada were rediscovered under the chapter house floor, where they had been placed in the 12th century. Even more remarkably, the exceptionally fine carved 12th–century grave slab, inscribed for Gundrada in black Tournai marble was found. This is now kept in a chapel dating from 1847 in the church of St John the Baptist, Southover, which started its life as the *hospitium* (guest house) at the north gate of the priory.

ABOVE: *View west down the shell of the huge 12th-century reredorter (latrine) building.*

Though a fragment of the south–west end of the great abbey church survives north of the railway line, the most impressive remains of the Cluniac priory lie to the south of the railway, hemmed in on their southern side by the Lewes bypass. Here we find the remains of the early 12th-century infirmary chapel, with unusual apsidal chapels on either side. This was systematically undermined and demolished, like the priory church, in 1537–8 by a specialist team of men under an Italian engineer called Giovanni Portinari, after Lewes had become the first of the greater priories to be dissolved on 11 November 1537.

South–west of the infirmary chapel are the impressive remains of the south–east side of the refectory building, to the east of which was the great dormitory. Attached to the dormitory's southern end by a bridge was a very large 12th-century building known as the 'reredorter'. This is a euphemism for the monks' common latrine, and the great size of the building is due to the fact that, under the rule of St Benedict, all the monks had 'to go to the toilet' (to use our modern euphemism) at the same time. Along the south–ern side of the reredorter can be seen the fixings for about 60 seats above a great east–west vaulted drain, which was flushed through with running water. This shows that by the middle of the 12th century there must have been about 60 monks at Lewes Priory, which was by this time the richest, as well as the earliest, Cluniac house in England.

Within the dormitory ruins to the north of the reredorter can still be seen the remains of an earlier, smaller reredorter (with only about 30 seats), which was superseded by and built into the extended dormitory. This must be the original monks' latrine built in the 1080s, and it is one of the oldest reredorters to survive in England (a much more fragmentary shell of a contemporary reredorter survives at Westminster Abbey).

In these ruins one can see clearly how rapidly Norman architecture was changing between the late 11th and mid 12th centuries. One can also see the ashlar masonry of Quarr stone from the Isle of Wight being replaced by Caen stone from Normandy.

Castle Acre Priory

CASTLE ACRE, NORFOLK

ABOVE: *View west down the shell of the reredorter. Note the broken arches which held the main floor above the stream.*

RIGHT: *The prior's house from the west. By the early 16th century it had its own grand entrance porch and oriel windows.*

This is the best–preserved Cluniac priory in England, and it forms the western part of one of the most interesting early medieval urban complexes in England, comparable with Lewes in East Sussex. To the east are a splendid early Norman castle and fortified town built by William de Warenne, one of William the Conqueror's most important and trusted followers, in the 1070s. It was at this castle that his wife Gundrada died in childbirth in 1085 (though she was buried at Lewes), by which time a small group of Cluniac monks was already established at Castle Acre. Just before William de Warenne's death in 1088 they must have started to build the eastern arm of the new priory church. This earliest part of the church, with apsidal chapels on its eastern side, can still be distinguished in the present ruins by its use of striped masonry (alternating courses of Barnack stone and the local brown Carr stone). By the early 12th century, when the work on the nave got under way, the Carr stone was no longer being used, and the rest of the fine nave and its western towers were finished by the mid 12th century in beautifully cut Barnack stone,

which was brought across the Fens from quarries north of Peterborough. Interestingly, one shipload of Caen stone from Normandy was also brought in, and this can be seen at one level, just above the west doorway, all around the west front.

Apart from its church, which had its east end demolished and extended in the early 14th century, Castle Acre priory still contains the ruins of many of its original 12th-century buildings around the cloister. These are the chapter house (originally with an apse) the first–floor dormitory and reredorter, the refectory, and the kitchen and cellarer's range. This last building was adapted and enlarged, from the late 12th century onwards, as the prior's house. By the early 16th century this was a very fine mansion indeed, and most of the western part of the building survived the Dissolution, when it became a farmhouse. The prior lived in great style, and one can still see his magnificent outer porch, with a study above it, and his first–floor private chapel and bedchamber, adorned with fine oriel windows and large inserted fireplaces. These were all built for Prior John Winchelsea, who also had a wooden long gallery built, although only traces of this now survive. His successor, Prior Thomas Malling, and ten monks were forced to surrender the priory to the duke of Norfolk on 22 November 1537, eleven days after Lewes Priory was handed over to the king's forces.

South–west of the main priory complex, a most interesting group of buildings around the outer court have been excavated and displayed. These comprise the later medieval kitchen, with a water mill to the west of it, both of which straddle the water–leat from the reredorter, and beyond this the stables, granaries and malthouses, with the bake-house and brewhouse complex to the south. The remains of several kilns and ovens, including the great oven where all the daily bread for the monks was made, can still be seen in these buildings, which are flanked by the River Nar on the southern side.

BELOW: *The view north-west across the cloister, to the ruined* cellarium. *Behind it is the prior's house and (on the right) the south-west tower of the church.*

LEFT: *The prior's bedroom or study in a fine upper room in his house. The splendid oriel window and fireplace were put in in the early 16th century. The doorway led to his chapel next door.*

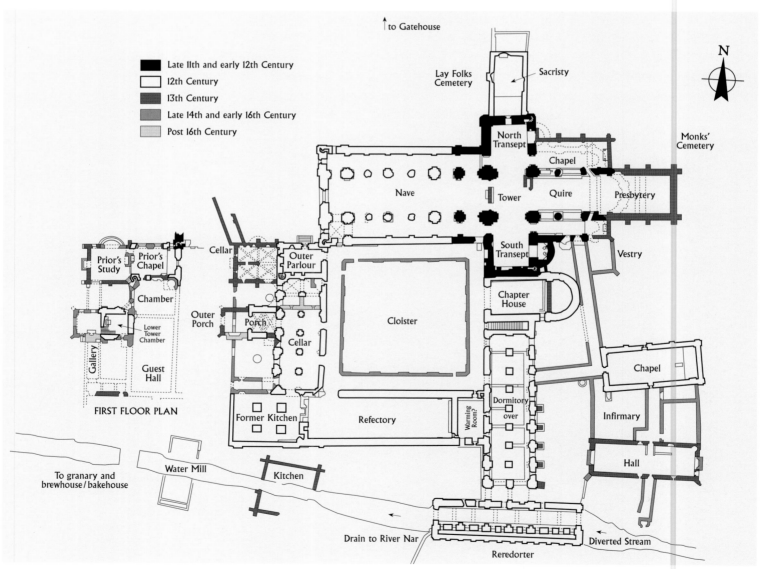

↑ to Gatehouse

Late 11th and early 12th Century
12th Century
13th Century
Late 14th and early 16th Century
Post 16th Century

N

Lay Folks Cemetery
Sacristy
Monks' Cemetery
North Transept
Chapel
Nave
Tower
Quire
Presbytery
Cellar
Outer Parlour
South Transept
Vestry
Prior's Study
Prior's Chapel
Chamber
Outer Porch
Porch
Cellar
Cloister
Chapter House
Lower Tower Chamber
Gallery
Guest Hall
FIRST FLOOR PLAN
Former Kitchen
Refectory
Warming Room?
Dormitory over
Chapel
Infirmary
Water Mill
Kitchen
Hall
To granary and brewhouse / bakehouse
Drain to River Nar
Reredorter
Diverted Stream

Thetford Priory

THETFORD, NORFOLK

HISTORY

- 1103 Priory started in old cathedral in town centre
- 1107 Priory moved to new site, building work starts
- Early 13th century – new Lady chapel built
- 1540 Dissolution of Priory

SPECIAL FEATURES

- Ruins of 12th century and later church
- Ruins of 13th-century Lady chapel and new eastern arm
- Foundations of 12th-century and later claustral buildings
- Shell of prior's house

ABOVE: *Corbelled head stop, beside a 12th-century archway in the later prior's house.*

RIGHT: *The inner (south) face of the large 14th-century gatehouse, which can be seen to the north of the church.*

I n the late Anglo–Saxon period Thetford was one of the largest towns in England, occupying a large area to the south of the Little Ouse. After the Norman Conquest the East Anglian cathedral was moved here from Elmham. It was transferred to Norwich after about 20 years in 1094, and a new motte–and–bailey castle was built north of the river, with a planned extension of the town to the west. Despite these developments, in the 12th century Thetford was superseded by Norwich as the chief town of the region – but not before a large new Cluniac priory had been built to the west of the Norman town.

The founder of the priory was Roger Bigod. He was one of William the Conqueror's powerful supporters, whose son Hugh became the first Earl of Norfolk. Roger Bigod first founded his priory in the old cathedral church in the centre of the town in 1103–04, with 12 monks from Lewes Priory. The site was too cramped, however, and they soon moved to the present site, outside the town, where they started to build the eastern arm of the present church on 1 September 1107, just before Roger Bigod died. The church and the first monastic buildings were rapidly built (as at Lewes and Castle Acre), and the lowest parts of these buildings can still be seen. They were all in use by the mid

ABOVE: *View north-west across the cloister garth from the warming house in the dormitory undercroft. In the distance are the remains of the prior's house, which was rebuilt after the Dissolution.*

12th century, and follow the usual pattern around the cloister: chapter house, dormitory, refectory and kitchen; with the cellarer's range on the west. Beyond the south end of the dormitory is the reredorter (latrine), and to the east the infirmary (around a miniature cloister) was added in the later 12th century. It is interesting to note that, as at Castle Acre, the apsidal eastern end of the chapter house was knocked off in the 14th century and replaced with a straight wall with fine knapped flintwork on the outside. The 12th-century eastern arcade was, however, reset against the new wall. The north end of the west range probably became the prior's house in the 13th century, and this must have been greatly enlarged in the late middle ages, again as at Castle Acre. It runs west from the west front of the church, but beyond this, unfortunately, its form is difficult to work out because only the shell of the building survives.

In the early part of the 13th century a large new Lady chapel was added to the north-east side of the church (as at Ely Cathedral) after miracles were recorded associated with the image of the Virgin. This was expanded westwards and southwards into a large new presbytery in the later 13th century. In the late Middle Ages, some of the Mowbrays (dukes of Norfolk) chose to be buried here, and the remains of what is probably the tomb of the last Mowbray duke (d. 1476) can be seen in the south choir aisle. After this the title and estates went to the Howards. The first of these dukes was killed in 1485 at the battle of Bosworth, where he fought for Richard III, and although he was first buried at Leicester, his body was later brought here for reburial. Various other fine monuments were made for the Howards, but only the remains of the burial vaults in the eastern arm can be seen today. After the Dissolution in 1540, the later burials were translated to Framlingham church, near the family seat at Framlingham castle.

To the north-west of the ruins can be seen the shell of the large northern gatehouse. To the west, some of the abbey barns survive in what is now the council depot.

Wenlock Priory

MUCH WENLOCK, SHROPSHIRE

HISTORY

- Late 7th century – First monastery founded at Wenlock
- c.1080 New Cluniac priory founded at Much Wenlock
- 1102 Becomes a Royal priory
- Early 13th century – church rebuilt
- 1395 Becomes an 'English' priory
- 1540 Dissolution of priory

SPECIAL FEATURES

- Remains of 12th–century chapter house and Lavatorium
- Ruins of large early 13th–century church
- Surviving prior's house to the south–east
- 12th–century Water Mill
- Well-preserved range of monastic buildings

ABOVE: *Looking east up the south aisle of the nave. The quadripartite rib-vaults still survive at the west end of the aisle.*

RIGHT: *The fine 13th-century doorway into the refectory from the south-western corner of the cloister.*

A monastery was first founded in this area, on the northern edge of the beautiful south Shropshire hills, at the end of the 7th century by Merewald, a member of the royal house of Mercia. Initially it was a 'double' house, with a nunnery and a community of priests living in two separate establishments alongside each other. The first abbess was Milburga, the founder's daughter. Fragments of what may have been one of these early churches have been found by excavation below the present ruined church, but it is possible that the site of the original church was at the parish church, a few hundred metres to the south–west. The early monastery was destroyed by the Vikings in the late 9th century, and the monastic site seems to have remained derelict until Leofric, Earl of Mercia, and his well–known wife, Lady Godiva, refounded the Minster at Wenlock around 1050. It is possible that part of the fabric of Leofric's church still survives in the present parish church of the Holy Trinity.

After the Norman Conquest Earl Roger of Montgomery founded a new Cluniac priory here, with monks bought over from one of the leading Cluniac houses, La–Charité–sur–Loire, dubbed the 'eldest daughter of Cluny'. This took place c.1079–82, and the new house was dedicated to St Milburga. The foundations of the three eastern apses of the late 11th-century church have been excavated beneath the 13th–century choir, but the earliest surviving building on the site is the ruined mid 12th–century chapter house. The base of the large octagonal lavatorium also probably dates from this time. In 1102 Wenlock became a royal priory, and was greatly enriched as a result, though its use by

ABOVE: *The substantial remains of the south transept seen from across the cloister garth. In the foreground are the remains of the 12th-century lavatorium, with beyond it the arched entrance to the chapter house.*

several kings for their own hospitality was an inevitable drain on its resources. A small town grew up around the priory, and in the early 13th century the church was rebuilt on a grand scale, as can be seen from the large 'chunks' of ruins that survive today – the magnificent aisled north and south transepts, and the south-west part of the nave, where three vaulted bays (with a room above) of the south aisle still survive.

By the later 13th century there were 44 monks here, but trouble arose when relations between England and France deteriorated. Only in 1395 did the priory officially become 'English', though the first English prior was appointed in 1376, and ties with the great French abbey at Cluny were not finally severed until 1494; it was the prior who finally achieved this, Richard Singer (1486–1521), who built the magnificent new prior's lodging to the south-east. This splendid building, which also incorporates the earlier infirmary hall and chapel, survives intact, and is still today a very fine private house.

St Mary's Abbey

READING, BERKSHIRE

SPECIAL FEATURES

- Ruins of south transept near grave site of Henry I
- Large ruined walls of chapter house, dormitory and reredorter
- Rebuilt inner gatehouse
- Fragment of mill on the Holy Brook (to the south)

ABOVE: *The remains of the large apsidal chapel to the east of the south transept.*

RIGHT: *The large inner gateway, rebuilt in 1861 after a partial collapse. Jane Austen attended school here for a time in 1784.*

Reading, one of the great royal abbeys of England, was founded in 1121 by King Henry I, youngest son of William the Conqueror, as a place of burial for him and his family. The site chosen was on the banks of the River Kennet, a short distance west of where it joined the Thames. Immediately to the west of the precinct was the small Berkshire market town of Reading, which would have benefited greatly from having a large new abbey beside it. Henry I asked the abbey of Cluny in Burgundy to help him set up his new monastery, and it duly sent eight monks, along with some others from Lewes Priory. They arrived on 18 June 1121, and for the first two years, while the work on the new church was starting, Reading was only a priory (the prior, Peter, came from Cluny). Then, on 15 April 1132, Hugh of Amiens (formerly prior of Lewes) was appointed the first abbot, and the prior returned to Cluny. The new monastery had, therefore, begun as a Cluniac priory, but now became a completely independent royal abbey.

A very large church, 450 feet long, was erected in the first half of the 12th century with a splendid cloister to the south. Sadly, most traces of the church have now gone, and the site of the eastern Lady chapel lies beneath the main gate to Reading prison – most famous, or infamous, as the place of Oscar Wilde's incarceration. The shells of the south transept (with an eastern apsidal chapel), and of the chapter house (also apsidal) can, however, still be seen, along with the ruins of the great dormitory and reredorter. All these structures display the flint-work rubble masonry of the earlier 12th century. The principal buildings of the abbey were complete by April 1164, when

ABOVE: *An atmospheric view down the east cloister walk to the River Kennet. On the left are the flint ruins of the west walls of the chapter house and dormitory.*

Archbishop Thomas Becket came to dedicate them. Henry I's probable place of burial, in the presbytery, is now covered by a Victorian Roman Catholic school, and all the remains are overshadowed by the high western wall of the prison. West of these ruins are some fine public gardens, called the Forbury Gardens; this was the area of the abbey's nave and outer court; the principal outer gates on the west and north–west have been destroyed, but the very fine inner gatehouse (heavily restored) still survives to the south. It probably led from the outer court to the palatial late medieval abbot's house. Several kings sought accommodation at this royal abbey, and in 1464 King Edward IV was married in the abbey church.

North and east of the Forbury Gardens and prison was the abbey's outer boundary wall, later called the Plumbery wall. This overlooked the water-meadows beside the Thames (now obscured by the tracks of Brunel's Great Western Railway), and in 1642 the walls were strengthened with earthworks during the Civil War.

The last abbot, Hugh Faringdon, and two monks bravely refused to accept the Dissolution in September 1539 and were taken off to the Tower of London. They were brought back to Reading on 13 November, hastily tried and convicted of treason. They were executed the following day, just outside the main gate; the abbey was quickly suppressed and pulled down. Only the abbot's house remained, as a royal residence, until 1642.

WHITE MONKS
(Cistercians)

Because they were sited in remote and 'barren' locations the ruins of the abbeys of the Cistercian Order are today some of the most beautiful and evocative places in England. Most sites were quickly developed through the hard work of the lay brothers (who did the physical work alongside the monks), and by the late middle ages many of them were rich estates producing wool; some, such as Fountains and

Furness, were very rich.

Cîteaux Abbey, Burgundy, (which gave its name to the Order) was founded in 1098. A much more austere regime than that of the Benedictines was quickly established there. Many people flocked to join the Order, the most famous and influential being Bernard of Fontaines (later St Bernard), who was the founding abbot of Clairvaux from 1115 until his death in 1153.

ABOVE: *Inscription at the top of the abbot's tower porch at Forde, recording that Thomas Chard made it in 1528.*

BELOW: *Looking west down the vast (over 200 feet long) nave at Fountains Abbey.*

Waverley Abbey

FARNHAM, SURREY

HISTORY

- 1128 Foundation by Bishop William Giffard
- c.1160 Start of enlargement of monastic buildings
- 1203–87 Very large new church built
- c.1500 cloister floors raised by three feet
- 1536 Abbey dissolved
- 1898–1902 Site excavated

SPECIAL FEATURES

- Shell of 13th-century church
- Shell of chapter house
- Ruins of southern ends of monks' and lay brothers' dormitories

ABOVE: *Looking south-west from the east end of the ruined abbey church to the ruins of the south transept.*

OPPOSITE TOP: *View south down the monks' dormitory which was extended southwards in the early 13th century.*

OPPOSITE BOTTOM: *The southern end of the vaulted undercroft of the lay brothers' dormitory. The central shafts and capitals are in polished Purbeck marble, though the abaci are of Wealden marble.*

The ruins of Waverley, the earliest Cistercian abbey in Britain, lie in the beautiful water-meadows by a loop in the river Wey, two miles south-east of the bishop of Winchester's castle and town of Farnham. These meadows, still surrounded by dense woodland on the sandy hills all around, are often flooded in winter, and repeated serious inundations forced the monks to raise the floor levels of the monastic buildings several times.

The founder of the abbey was William Giffard, bishop of Winchester from 1107 to 1129, who brought monks here in 1128 from the French Abbey of l'Aumône (a daughter house of Cîteaux). They quickly built a small church and the main claustral buildings, and the lower walls and floors of these earliest parts of the abbey were uncovered in the large-scale excavations carried out between 1898 and 1902 by W. H. St John Hope and Harold Brakspear. Because of the flooding, the lower archaeological levels were buried and well preserved, but today they have been covered up again. By the later 12th century the abbey had expanded hugely, and in 1187 there were 70 choir monks and 120 lay brothers. To accommodate them, the east and south ranges were rebuilt and expanded between about 1160 and 1180. None of these buildings are now visible, except the shell of the large rectangular chapter house, which had benches around the walls. One can also see fragments of the polished Wealden marble bases for the elaborate shafting used in the chapter house. Next to it on the south side is a barrel-vaulted passage that led from the cloister to the infirmary. To the south again lay the large dormitory. This was extended on two occasions; on the second, in the early 13th century, the shell that survives today was built, with its three large lancets in the south wall overlooking the river. To the west are the rib-vaulted ruins of a contemporary dormitory for the lay brothers.

In 1203 work began on building a large new abbey church, with a series of chapels on the eastern sides of the presbytery and transepts. This was built to the north of the old church, and after delays during King John's chaotic reign, the monks were eventually able to move into the new eastern arm (choir and presbytery) in 1231. The old church was then demolished, although the rebuilding of the nave and enlargement of the cloister took another half-century. Only fragments of the outer walls of the great church now survive (with a magnificent great yew tree sitting on the south-east corner), but the south transept has in its walls traces of both the early and the later churches.

After the Dissolution in 1536 part of the abbey was turned into a house, but this was demolished in 1725, when a large new house was built outside the abbey precinct to the north. This house and its grounds can still be seen beyond the serpentine pond to the north, which may originally have been made from the monastic fishponds.

Forde Abbey

CHARD, SOMERSET

HISTORY

- 1133 Foundation at Brightley
- 1141 Move to Forde
- 1239 Abbey church dedicated
- 1521–39 Much rebuilding by Abbot Chard
- 1539 Abbey dissolved
- 1650 Rebuilding of house

SPECIAL FEATURES

- Mid 12th-century chapter house
- 13th-century dormitory range
- Abbot Chard's tower porch and great hall
- Early 16th-century north cloister walk, with fragment of 13th-century lavatorium

ABOVE: *The corridor down the west side of the lay brothers' dormitory, with its 19th-century plaster vault below a medieval roof.*

RIGHT: *Abbot Chard's magnificent great hall and tower porch, seen from the south-west. They are flanked by the rebuilt 17th-century parts of the house.*

OPPOSITE: *The splendid great hall of Abbot Chard's palatial residence.*

Two miles north of Okehampton, on the north side of Dartmoor in mid-Devon, is a remote site in the Okement valley called Brightley. Here in 1133 Richard fitz Baldwin de Brionne, lord of Okehampton, decided to settle a group of Cistercian monks from Waverley. A superior and 12 monks arrived on 3 May 1136 and started to build the new monastery; but their founder died in 1137, and they found the site just too harsh, even for Cistercians. So in 1141 they moved to a new site at the meeting point between Devon, Dorset and Somerset at Forde (in Thorncombe parish, now in Dorset, but then part of Devon). Here they succeeded, and a new set of buildings was erected by the River Axe in the mid-12th century under Abbot Robert de Pennington (1137–68), though only the fine rib-vaulted chapter house of the abbey (now the post-medieval chapel) survives from his time. The next abbot, Baldwin (1168–81), was an exceptional man, who had met and been inspired by St Bernard of Clairvaux and the Cistercian Pope, Eugenius III, in Rome. He brought Forde to what must have been its peak, with over 60 monks and many more lay brothers, before he moved on to be bishop of Worcester and archbishop of Canterbury. He died in the Holy Land on the Third Crusade in 1190.

By the 13th century Forde was a large and flourishing Cistercian abbey, and from

ABOVE: *The very fine 13th-century undercroft in the lay brothers' range, with its chequered ribs of Ham Hill stone and Bath stone.*

this period we have the magnificent surviving lay brothers' dormitory range on its fine rib-vaulted undercroft, 170 feet long, with 12 bays. Down the centre is a row of octagonal piers, and at the northern end was the drain for the reredorter – appropriately enough, where the modern WCs are now!) An early wall painting of Christ on the Cross, with Mary and John, has recently been uncovered in the northern section of the undercroft. The upper west wall of the dormitory still contains the 13 lancet windows that lit the dormitory itself, which lay above the undercroft.

The church at Forde, which has been completely demolished (its foundations now lie under the front lawns), was dedicated in 1239 by the bishop of Exeter, in whose diocese it lay, and the cloister and monastic buildings were on the north side of the church. The 13th-century refectory and kitchen still survive to the north of the north cloister walk, but were shortened and rebuilt in the 15th century, when the number of monks had dropped and the Cistercian order was no longer at its peak. The endowments of the abbey were still very great, however, and the last abbot, Thomas Chard (1521–39), spent huge sums on rebuilding the abbey and constructing a palatial residence for himself. Chard, a prominent Cistercian administrator, attended the great chapter meet-

ABOVE: *The mid 12th-century chapter house (now the chapel) looking east to its fine early 16th-century east window and 17th-century screen.*

ABOVE RIGHT: *The unfinished early 16th-century north cloister walk, with its 19th-century plaster vault.*

ings at Cîteaux in 1515 and 1518; he must have seen something of the new Renaissance style on his European travels, and it is the remarkable Renaissance decoration on his amazing house at Forde that has survived at the core of the present building. First there is a wonderful three-storied porch with an oriel window on it (dated 1528); this leads to a huge new great hall (seven bays and 83 feet long). To the east of the porch was Chard's first-floor great chamber, but this was rebuilt in the mid-17th century. All this work is in the very handsome stone from Ham Hill, where the abbot had leased a quarry since 1478 at 4d a year. Chard also rebuilt the cloister, and his beautiful – though unfinished – north walk can still be seen. Many other buildings were no doubt reconstructed as well: John Leland, who saw the work just before the Dissolution, tells us that the 'abbot at incredible expense is now restoring the monastery most gloriously'. In March 1539 Abbot Chard and 12 monks surrendered the house, and it was then sold to a succession of owners. In 1649 the house was bought by Sir Edmund Prideaux, a wealthy lawyer and MP who became Oliver Cromwell's Solicitor General; he rebuilt it in the 1650s in the style of Inigo Jones. This is now the house that survives, in a magnificent garden setting.

Jervaulx Abbey

NEAR LAYBURN, NORTH YORKSHIRE

HISTORY

- 1145 Founded at Fors
- 1156 Move to present site
- Late 12th–13th centuries – much rebuilding work
- 15th century – rebuilding in area of abbot's lodging
- 1537 Dissolution of abbey and execution of abbot

SPECIAL FEATURES

- Ruins of many monastic buildings 'hidden' in vegetation
- Shells of monks' dormitory and chapter house
- Remains of large abbey church on the north

ABOVE: *View north-east through one of the chapter house windows to one of the piers that originally supported the vaulted ceiling.*

RIGHT: *The north wall of the monks' infirmary, built in the later 13th century. The main hall was above the vaulted undercroft.*

Jervaulx is one of the very few remaining privately–owned abbeys. It is maintained as a picturesque 'romantic' ruin on the edge of the garden of the 17th–century Jervaulx Hall, reached by walking through sheep–grazed parkland. The ruined site was dug out as early as 1805 by John Claridge for the then owner, the Earl of Ailesbury. More uncovering took place in 1905–7 under W. H. St John Hope and Harold Brakspear.

The abbey was first established in 1145 at Fors, some 16 miles to the west, by a community of Savigniac monks. By 1156 they had moved to the present site above the River Ure: hence the medieval name for the abbey, Joreval ('Ure Vale'). The French–sounding 'Jervaulx' was a 19th–century imposition. As in so many monastic foundations, much of the building work was rapidly done in the middle to later 12th century, particularly under Abbot John of Kinstan, as the numbers of monks and lay brothers increased. At the end of the 12th century the church was greatly enlarged; it is still possible to distinguish parts of the early and later south walls of the church in the south transept.

The site on which the visitor enters through the gate from the park is very confusing, with masses of architectural fragments from the 1805 dig piled up everywhere. This

ABOVE: *The doorway in the south-west corner of the nave through which the lay brothers entered the church from the night staircase.*

RIGHT: *The magnificent west wall of the monks' dormitory from the north-east. The large opening on the right contained the day stair doorway.*

ABOVE: *The abbey ruins seen from the south-east with the ruins of the monks' infirmary in the centre. The abbot's lodging was to the left.*

south–west corner of the abbey was where the lay brothers' quarters were situated, and the walls are not well preserved. However, if one crosses these to the neat lawn in the cloister garth it becomes easy to orientate oneself, with the great church to the north and the shell of the chapter house (with its six monolithic columns) to the east. Little survives of the walls of the church, but its plan can be easily made out. At the east end were five stone altars on raised platforms, with a further two in each of the transepts. The western part of the nave contained the lay brothers' choir, and at its south–west corner is a well-preserved doorway which led directly to the night stairs, outside the extreme north end of the lay brothers' dormitory.

South–east of the cloister are the well-preserved ruins of the large west wall of the monks' dormitory. The row of nine tall lancets is particularly impressive. East of this are the complicated ruins of the reredorter, great kitchen, infirmary and abbot's house, all covered in vegetation. The huge fireplaces in the large, square kitchen (dating from the later medieval period) can, however, be identified, as can the remains of the vaulted undercroft of the 13th–century monks' infirmary. To the north is the deep drain below the monks' reredorter.

Jervaulx's last abbot, Adam Sedbar, was directly involved in the 'Pilgrimage of Grace', the revolt against Henry VIII's church reforms. As a result the abbey was suppressed in 1537; the abbot was executed, and the buildings were demolished.

Rievaulx Abbey

NEAR HELMSLEY, NORTH YORKSHIRE

HISTORY

- 1132 Founding of abbey
- 1147–67 Enlargement of abbey by abbot Aelred
- 1180 Large new refectory built
- Early 13th century – eastern arm of church rebuilt
- 1538 – Dissolution of monastery

SPECIAL FEATURES

- Ruins of 12th–century nave and large 13th–century eastern arm of church
- Shell of large refectory
- Unique 12th–century chapter house, with shrine of St William
- Excavated ruins of many monastic buildings

ABOVE: *The remains of the mid 13th-century tomb-shrine of the first abbot, William, beside the main door into the chapter house, from the cloister.*

RIGHT: *The magnificent shell of the monks' refectory seen from the south-west. Behind it is the gable top of the south transept.*

This was probably the most important and influential Cistercian abbey in Britain, founded only a few years after Waverley. The surviving ruins are exceptionally well preserved, and lie within a very beautiful setting in the Rye valley – from which its French name derives. The first monks were mostly Yorkshire men who had gone to St Bernard's famous abbey at Clairvaux, and had then been sent back to start the Cistercian colonization of the north of England and Scotland. The first abbot was William, who had been Master of the Schools at York before going to France. At Clairvaux, he became secretary to Abbot Bernard (later Saint Bernard). In 1131 he left France for England with 12 monks, and was given a site for a new abbey by Walter Espec, lord of Helmsley (a Royal Justiciar of King Henry I). The monks arrived at the site, close to Helmsley castle, on 5 March 1132, and began building immediately. Within a year they were starting to establish daughter houses at Warden in Bedfordshire and at Melrose in Scotland, the latter being endowed by King David of Scotland.

The third abbot of Rievaulx, a former steward of King David, was called Aelred

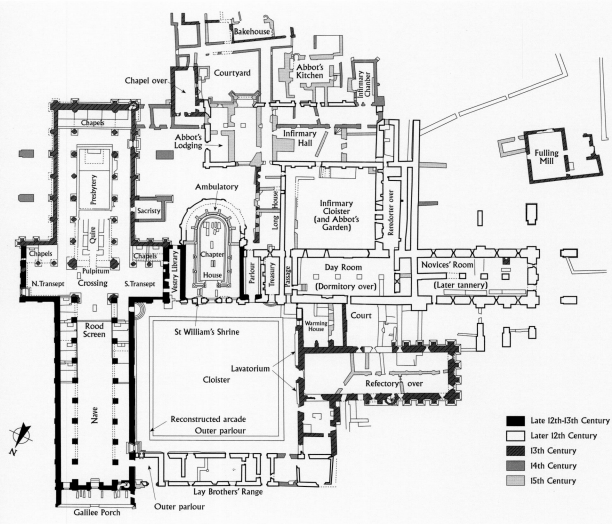

Late 12th-13th Century (black)
Later 12th Century (white)
13th Century (hatched)
14th Century (dark grey)
15th Century (light grey)

Labels on plan: Bakehouse, Chapel over, Courtyard, Abbot's Kitchen, Infirmary Chamber, Chapels, Abbot's Lodging, Infirmary Hall, Fulling Mill, Ambulatory, Sacristy, Presbytery, Long House, Infirmary Cloister (and Abbot's Garden), Reredorter over, Chapels, Quire, Chapter House, Parlour, Treasury, Passage, Day Room (Dormitory over), Novices' Room (Later tannery), N. Transept, Pulpitum, Crossing, S. Transept, Vestry library, Rood Screen, St William's Shrine, Warming House, Court, Lavatorium, Cloister, Refectory over, Nave, Reconstructed arcade, Outer parlour, Lay Brothers' Range, Galilee Porch, Outer parlour

OPPOSITE: *The south transept of the abbey church, with the remarkable eastern ambulatory of the chapter house in the foreground.*

(1147–67), and it was he who was responsible for putting up many of the buildings that still survive as the core of the ruins. This remarkable man, one of the greatest spiritual writers of western Christendom, became the most famous monk in England. After his death he was canonized, and a new shrine was created for St Aelred in the magnificent new Gothic eastern arm of the church that was created in the early 13th century. Much of this splendid addition survives, though all traces of the shrine itself have gone. The nave, by contrast, though less well preserved, is still the very austere structure put in place by Aelred. Immediately to the south of the south transept is Aelred's extraordinary apsidal chapter house. Unlike any other chapter house, it had an ambulatory all around the outside separated from the chapter house itself by large circular piers. At the cloister ends of the outer passageway there were separate doorways, and it is possible that this ambulatory was used by the lay brothers when they came to listen to the sermons in the chapter house. With the disappearance of the lay brothers after the Black Death, the eastern part of the ambulatory was demolished and the arches in the semicircular apse were filled up. The floor of the chapter house contained the grave slabs of many of the abbots, and on the north side of the entrance doorway are the remains of the mid 13th-century tomb-shrine of the first abbot, St William (1132–45).

Many other of the monastic buildings are preserved as impressive ruins: the finest of all is the huge late 12th-century monks' refectory, built down the hill on a very large undercroft. It stands at right angles to the south side of the cloister and was entered by a fine central doorway, flanked by the remains of a lavatorium (where the monks washed their hands, and on a Saturday each others' feet, following the example of Christ). By the time the refectory was rebuilt, there were 140 choir monks at Rievaulx and over 500 lay brothers and lay servants. When the abbey was suppressed in 1538 the lay brothers had gone, but there were still 102 paid servants attending to a very grand abbot (living in a magnificent house on the south-east part of the monastery) and just 22 monks.

Fountains Abbey

NEAR RIPON, NORTH YORKSHIRE

HISTORY

- 1132 Founding of abbey
- 1150 Building of present church
- 1539 Final suppression of abbey by Henry VIII
- 1768 Incorporated into landscaped parkland of Studley Royal

SPECIAL FEATURES

- 'Hammerhead' east end – the chapel of the Nine Altars
- 170-ft church bell tower added to the north transept in *c.*1520
- Spectacular vaulted cellarium
- 12th-century water mill, used until 1937
- Many well-preserved monastic buildings

ABOVE: *West view from the reredorter to the well-preserved refectory.*

OPPOSITE: *View north-east across the wonderful 'Nine Altars' chapel. All the polished columns of Nidderdale marble have been removed.*

his is probably the most famous and magnificent ruined abbey in Britain. The site was first settled by a group of monks from St Mary's Abbey in York, who wanted a much stricter regime. They had no doubt seen the Clairvaux monks passing through York early in 1132 on their way to found Rievaulx, and after much dissent they persuaded Archbishop Thurstan of York (1114–40) to be their patron and protector. At the very end of 1132 he led them to Ripon and gave them a wild site on the River Skell, a few miles to the west of the town. Here they spent a difficult winter, but in 1133 their first abbot, Richard (1132–9) was allowed to affiliate his monks to the Cistercian order, and Bernard of Clairvaux sent Geoffrey d'Ainai from Rievaulx to help them put up their first, temporary, timber buildings. Remarkably, the post-hole remains of these buildings (and the 1135 foundations of the first stone church) were found in an excavation in the south transept in 1980. The present large church was built under the fourth main abbot, another Richard (1150–70), in the 1150s, and much of the nave of this fine but austere building remains intact, with unusual transverse barrel vaults over the aisles. Two-thirds of the nave was originally used by the hundreds of lay brothers who came to work at the abbey in the latter years of the 12th century, but in the later middle ages, after the departure of these men, the aisles were filled with a whole series of altars. The eastern arm of the church was wonderfully rebuilt in the first half of the 13th century. The famous 'hammer-head' east end, holding nine altars, was put up under Abbot John of Kent (1220–47), and was originally filled with a very large number of polished Nidderdale marble shafts. Alas, only a few fragments of these remain. The final, and equally unusual, addition to the church was the magnificent 170-foot-high bell tower that was added to the north transept by Abbot Marmaduke Huby (1495–1526), perhaps the greatest of all Fountains' abbots. A great reformer, he gave the abbey its final prosperity in the early Tudor period, when it was the richest Cistercian monastery in Britain. When the abbey was finally dissolved at the end of 1539, Henry VIII was thinking of turning this great church into a new cathedral for Richmondshire, but this never happened. Three hundred years later, nearby Ripon Minster became a cathedral.

The surviving monastic buildings to the south of the great church are equally impressive. To the west of the great cloister is the largest and best-preserved lay brothers' range in Europe, with beneath it the spectacular vaulted cellarium, over 300 feet long. West of this are the shells of the lay brothers' reredorter and infirmary, all cleverly built over the River Skell. Beyond are two large guest houses, and a malt house and wool house (wool was the principal source of Fountains' great wealth). There are also two fine medieval bridges over the river, and a 12th-century water mill that was in use until 1937.

ABOVE: *The Chapel of the Nine Altars seen from the ruins of the infirmary hall to the south-east.*

BELOW: *View south down the vast cellarium in the west range.*

Returning to the great cloister, we find the well–preserved remains of the chapter house and the monks' refectory and dormitory. Between these two later buildings is the dormitory day stair, which also leads up to the still vaulted muniment room where documents were kept over the warming house. The large fireplaces on the east still have a great cylindrical chimney above them. Passing under the dormitory from the south–east corner of the cloister, one reaches a large, formerly covered, passageway which leads to Abbot John of Kent's huge infirmary hall (also built across the river on four great tunnel–vaults), chapel and kitchens. Side doors out of this long passageway lead to the chapel of the Nine Altars (north) and the abbot's house (south).

ABOVE: *View towards the 12th-century infirmary bridge and west and east guest houses, with the Skell below.*

The 73-acre abbey precinct was surrounded by a large stone wall, and much of this survives on the south and west (to the north was a long cliff in places). Within it were the cemetery, gardens, fishponds and orchards, as well as many other buildings, yet to be uncovered, and a whole series of water pipes and tanks, which gave the abbey constant running water from the fine hillside springs (hence its name). The abbey was suppressed in 1539, and in 1768 the whole of the former abbey site was incorporated into the landscaped parkland of Studley Royal, ensuring at an early date the survival of the buildings as landscape features. These are all now owned by the National Trust, which bought the whole estate as recently as 1983.

Croxden Abbey

UTTOXETER, STAFFORDSHIRE

HISTORY

- 1176 Abbey founded at Cotton
- 1179 move to present site
- 1220 start of work on new abbey church
- 1335 new abbot's lodging started
- 1538 Dissolution of abbey

SPECIAL FEATURES

- Fragment of 'chevet' of eastern arm
- South transept and west front of abbey church
- Remains of chapter house and dormitory undercroft

ABOVE: *Part of the north wall of the chapter house, glimpsed though its doorway.*

RIGHT: *Worn, headless sculpture of a cross-legged knight from a tomb in the church.*

I n Staffordshire, some 5 miles north–west of Uttoxeter, lie the ruins of Croxden, a daughter house of the Savigniac abbey of Aulnay–sur–Odon in Normandy. The abbey was initially established, in 1176, a few miles to the north of Croxden at Cotton (near what is now Alton Towers), by a group of French monks on land given by Bertram de Verdun, who died at Acre in 1192 while on the Third Crusade with Richard Cœur de Lion. In 1179, however, the monks moved south to the vale of the Croxden brook, where work on a new foundation started slowly under their first abbot, an Englishman called Thomas of Woodstock. Under Thomas, who remained abbot for over 50 years, the monks soon built up a new community and started to erect stone buildings. When Abbot Thomas died in 1229 and was buried in the chapter house, work was under way on a new enlarged eastern arm, with unusual radiating chapels in the French style. Unfortunately, after the Dissolution a road was built diagonally across the church, and only a small fragment of one radiating

chapel can now be seen to the north of the road. By contrast, however, much of the tall south wall of the south transept still survives, as does the buttressed west wall of the aisled nave, with its very tall triple lancets and finely moulded doorway. The eastern arm was consecrated in 1232, but more rebuilding took place after this on the church, which was finally dedicated in 1254 under Abbot Walter of London (1242–68). He also enlarged the chapter house, built a north–south refectory in the south cloister range and extended the dormitory range. The foundations of the main buildings around the cloister have been uncovered, but a post-medieval farmhouse lies across the south-west corner of the cloister area. Surprisingly, there does not seem to have been an early lay brothers' dormitory and refectory in the west range, but more excavation is needed to clarify the earliest phases of the monastery. We know from documentary evidence that all the cloister buildings were covered in shingles; only in

ABOVE: *The south transept end wall and the chapter house, seen through a tree-filled gap in the south wall of the nave.*

1332–4 were they recovered in lead. A new abbot's lodging was built for Abbot Richard Shepshed to the south-east in the following year (1335–6), so the abbey had clearly become more prosperous again just before the Black Death. By the late middle ages, the abbot's house had expanded northwards into the old infirmary building, and when the abbey was surrendered on 17 September 1538, only the abbot and 12 monks remained.

Around the abbey ruins are various earthwork remains within a large rectangular precinct. Beside the principal northern gatehouse is a surviving gate-chapel of the later 13th century. There is also a large millpond and dam, with another larger millpond beyond. The abbey's main wealth must, however, have come from its large herds of sheep in the north Staffordshire area.

Roche Abbey

MALTBY, SOUTH YORKSHIRE

SPECIAL FEATURES

- Eastern arm of church
- Ruins of nave, claustral buildings and abbot's house
- c.1170 vaulted gatehouse

ABOVE: *Looking south-east into the precinct through the fine vaulted outer gatehouse of the 1170s*

OPPOSITE: *The view east-wards from the north side of the nave to the magnificent east elevations of the 1160s transepts.*

Roche Abbey took its French name from the rocky cliff in the Magnesian limestone to the north of the abbey, cut out by the Maltby Beck. The monastery was founded in 1147 as a daughter house of Newminster Abbey in Northumberland, and was hence a 'grand-daughter' of Fountains. It lies 13 miles east of Sheffield in the valley of Maltby Beck. Most of the lowest walls of the main buildings can still be seen, having been dug out in 1870. A century earlier the upstanding ruins (only the eastern part of the church) had been incorporated into a series of a grass parterres laid out by the great garden designer Lancelot (Capability) Brown, as part of his landscaping of Sandbeck Park.

The surviving ruins of the eastern part of the church are of particular interest, as they are some of the earliest remains showing the transition from the late Romanesque to the earliest Gothic in England. The plan of the east end of the church is typical of an early Cistercian church, with a simple square sanctuary flanked by pairs of square-ended chapels in the transepts. However, the elevations have pointed arches into the chapels, and there are also pointed arches in the blind arcade of the triforium above. Only in the top storey, where the scars for the ribbed vaults can be seen, are the openings still round-headed. One gets the impression that the design was being worked out while the building was going up in the later 1160s under Abbot Dionysius (1159–71). The monks' choir was to the west of the crossing, and one can see the remains of the base of the screen to the west of this that separated off the lay brothers' nave.

Most of the monastic buildings were put up (and some of them then enlarged) under Abbot Osmund (1184–1213), who had been the cellarer at Fountains Abbey. The cloister is south of the nave, with the sacristy and library, and then the chapter house, in the east walk. Further south was the dormitory undercroft, which was later extended across the Maltby Beck. South-east of it are the reredorter and infirmary cloister. The buildings to the south of this were converted into the abbot's house in the late middle ages. South of the main cloister was the refectory (also extended over the beck), flanked by the warming house (east) and kitchen (west). The west range, as usual, was made for the lay brothers, who had their own infirmary across the Maltby Beck to the south. Beyond this was a large fishpond surrounded by abbey's precinct wall, much of which still survives. There is also a large vaulted 1170s gatehouse to the north-west of the abbey, and up the hill to the north are the remains of the quarry from which the fine building stone was obtained.

The abbey was surrendered on 23 June 1538, and soon afterwards was plundered by the local people. An eyewitness account tells us that 'All things of price were spoiled, carted away, or defaced to the uppermost . . . it seemeth that every person bent himself to filch and spoil what he could.'

Furness Abbey

BARROW–IN–FURNESS, CUMBRIA

ABOVE: *Detail of a fine decorated tomb-chest in the choir aisle.*

RIGHT: *View south-west from the early 13th-century chapter house, through its vestibule to the cloister.*

urness is the great peninsula on the south–west side of the Lake District, formerly part of Lancashire. The industrial town of Barrow that today lies just beyond the abbey had a fine natural harbour, guarded by the abbey's own castle. By the end of the Middle Ages Furness was the second richest Cistercian monastery in England, with very large estates extending north and north–eastwards into the heart of the Lake District, as well as others across Morecambe Bay in Lancashire and north–west Yorkshire.

The ruins lie in a beautiful valley (though the railway, complained about by Wordsworth, is a little too close for comfort!) where the monastery was established in 1127 by Stephen, count of Boulogne and Mortain, and later king of England (1135–54). Three years earlier, Stephen had given the original Savigniac monks a site at Tulketh near Preston; this proved unsuitable, and three years later the monks moved to Furness. In 1147 all the Savigniac foundations were amalgamated with the (by then very successful) Cistercian order, and Furness soon attracted very large numbers of extra monks and lay brothers. The magnificent surviving remains, made largely of the local New Red Sandstone, are some of the largest and most impressive monastic ruins in north–west England.

The abbey was built in a narrow and constricted north–south valley: hence the great church is not strictly oriented, and its 15th-century western bell-tower was squashed into the original west front. The outer and inner courts and principal gateways were on the north (the lowest walls of the great gatehouse are now beside the car park), and the site is entered through a modern museum on this side. After crossing neat lawns containing the insubstantial remains of the guest house and stables, one arrives at the principal 12th-century doorway into the church, which leads into the well-preserved

BELOW: *The five heavily moulded arches that led in to the chapter house and dormitory on the east side of the cloister.*

north transept. The eastern arm of the church stands almost to its full height, and one can see how the mid 12th-century structure was substantially rebuilt after subsidence problems in the late Middle Ages, when large new Perpendicular windows, and a monumental piscina and sedilia, were put in. Excavations in 1896–8 under W. H. St John Hope found the apsidal eastern chapels of the earliest Savigniac church. Across the transept from the north door, the night stair to the monks' dormitory can be seen, and beneath this are the great book cupboards that flank the vestibule to the once-vaulted chapter house, an impressive mid 13th-century building. The shell of the monks' dormitory and undercroft also survives, in contrast to the refectory and lay brothers' range on the west, where only the foundations can be seen. Further south are the foundations of the very large infirmary hall. Most of its east wall is still intact, with doors leading into the chapel and buttery. The latter is connected by a covered passageway with the octagonal kitchen. Beyond this, tucked into the hillside, is the earlier infirmary, which became the abbot's house in the later Middle Ages. Under many of these buildings run a series of watercourses (several of them still flowing) encased in masonry walls and vaults.

Outside the confines of the present site are the remains of other buildings, fishponds, a mill and stone quarries, all surrounded by a large precinct wall, and the remains of the outer gatehouses on the west and north (the latter with a chapel outside it). To the south-east, and on the Millbeck, is a fine three-arched 15th-century bridge, known as Bow Bridge ('bow' being the medieval name for an arch).

BELOW: The fine late 13th-century east wall of the infirmary hall, with the chapel on the right. The doorways on the left went to the buttery and kitchen.

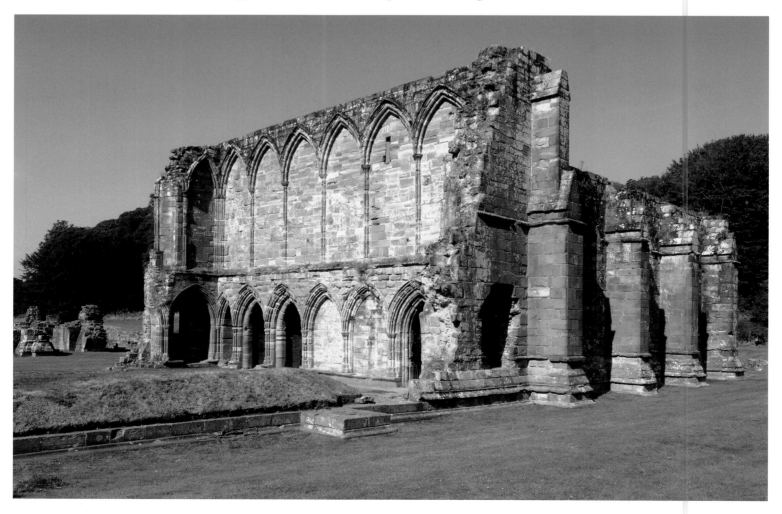

Hailes Abbey

WINCHCOMBE, GLOUCESTERSHIRE

HISTORY

- 1246 Foundation of new royal abbey
- 1251 Dedication of eastern arm of abbey church
- 1270 Shrine of Holy Blood dedicated
- 15th century – abbot's house rebuilt
- 1539 Dissolution of abbey

SPECIAL FEATURES

- Foundations of 'chevet' and shrine in eastern arm of church
- Remains of chapter house, dormitory and reredorter
- Foundations of abbot's house in west range
- Parish church (gatehouse chapel)

ABOVE: *Detail of a 15th-century angel corbel, beside a large cupboard in the north cloister walk.*

RIGHT: *Ruined late medieval arches in the west cloister walk, which were once joined to the abbots' house. The lavatorium and refectory doorway can be seen through the arch.*

O n 17 June 1246 a great service of dedication was held at Beaulieu Abbey in the New Forest to mark the completion of the great Cistercian abbey founded there by King John (with monks brought directly from Cîteaux) in 1204. This service was attended by King Henry III and many nobles and bishops, including the king's younger brother, Richard, earl of Cornwall (1209–72). On the previous day a foundation charter had been drawn up for a new royal Cistercian abbey at Hailes, 10 miles east of Tewkesbury at the foot of the Cotswolds. The site was on land given by the king to his brother, Earl Richard, so that he could fulfil a vow made in October 1242, when he was saved from drowning in a shipwreck. Immediately after the ceremony at Beaulieu, 20 monks and 10 lay brothers were sent to Hailes, and soon after their arrival on 23 June work started on a splendid

ABOVE: *The remains of the day stair to the monks' dormitory, which leads out of the south-east corner of the cloister.*

new monastery, with a great church 341 feet long. In the same year of 1246 Henry III began work on his vast new abbey church at Westminster, and it is therefore no coincidence that the plan of the remarkable 'chevet' (east end) at Hailes (with five radiating chapels) is exactly the same as that laid out at Westminster in 1246. Unfortunately, all that remain are the foundations of the buttressed walls of the five radiating chapels, with inside them the ambulatory passage marked today by the foundations of the moulded piers of the arcades. Between the piers would have been the tombs of Earl Richard's family, with the place of honour on the north side being for the earl himself. At the centre of all this is a rectangular base on which was situated the magnificent shrine of the Holy Blood, which contained a phial of the blood of Christ, acquired by Earl Richard in 1267, and 'authenticated' by Pope Urban IV, then the patriarch of Jerusalem. In the later middle ages, Hailes was a popular destination for pilgrims; but in November 1538 the phial of holy blood was taken to London and declared to be a fake by Bishop Hilsey of Rochester. The abbey itself was surrendered just over a year later, on Christmas Eve 1539.

Aside from the remains of the church itself, much of the plan of the abbey buildings was uncovered in the late 19th century. This can be related to the upstanding remains of the chapter house west wall and refectory north wall on the east and south sides of the cloister respectively. The north cloister walk also contains the niches for the monks' book-cupboards, and much of the surviving 13th-century masonry is in fine Cotswold stone, with decorated capitals, columns and bases in a grey-blue marble made of the local Blue Lias.

The remains of the wall foundations in the west range are much more complicated, because the lay brothers' accommodation here was converted into a large new abbot's house in the late Middle Ages. This continued in use, and was enlarged, after the Dissolution, and the whole building was still standing in the early 18th century, when it was set within a beautiful series of formal gardens. This house incorporated the 15th-century traceried arcades of the west cloister walk, and three of the arches remain standing. It was abandoned by the Tracey family who had lived there when they moved to another house at Toddington, 2 miles to the north, and soon afterwards was demolished.

Just to the north of the abbey is the earlier parish church of Hailes. When the abbey church was built it became a chapel outside the north gatehouse, and still contains some very fine early 14th-century wall paintings.

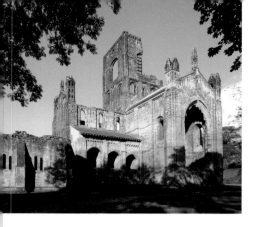

Kirkstall Abbey

LEEDS, WEST YORKSHIRE

HISTORY

- 1147 Foundation at Barnoldswick
- 1152 Move to Kirkstall, and start of work of present church
- 1182 Claustral buildings finished
- 13th century – Chapter house enlarged and abbot's lodging built
- 1539 Dissolution of abbey

SPECIAL FEATURES

- Shell of very complete abbey church
- Chapter house
- Remains of other monastic buildings
- Gatehouse and Museum

ABOVE: *The very impressive ruins of the abbey church from the south-east, with the east wall of the chapter house on the left.*

RIGHT: *The ruined walls of the late 13th-century abbot's lodging, seen from the south-west.*

The abbey church at Kirkstall is the best-preserved Cistercian church in Britain. Unfortunately, however, its beautiful situation by the River Aire was engulfed by the great city of Leeds in the 19th century, and now a major road runs right through the precinct, cutting off the gatehouse on the north from the rest of the abbey buildings. The monastic buildings do, however, still lie in a public park, given to the city in 1890.

In 1147 a group of 12 monks and 10 lay brothers under the first abbot, Alexander (1147–82), were sent out from Fountains Abbey to Barnoldswick to found a new abbey. This was to be Fountains' fifth daughter house, but unfortunately it failed, and in 1152 the new monastery was moved to Kirkstall. With the generous help of their patron, Henry de Lacy, they were soon successful, and the present abbey church was rapidly erected, the eastern arm being in use by 1159. There is a typical early Cistercian chancel, flanked by transepts, each with three chapels on its eastern side. The chapels are covered by pointed barrel vaults, but the chancel itself has two bays of early ribbed vaults over it, and one can see from the fabric how this was a change of plan from the barrel vault that it was originally intended to have. At Fountains the nave aisles have transverse barrel

ABOVE: *View north through the great 12th-century arches that separated the lay brothers' range (left) from the kitchen.*

BELOW: *A pair of lancets in the south wall of the extended vaulted chapter house.*

vaults, but here at Kirkstall quadripartite ribbed vaults are used, showing how the later Romanesque architecture was developing at this time. The nave, completed by about 1170, ends in an externally gabled west doorway. The main windows (especially the east window) in the church were replaced in the late middle ages, but evidence still survives of an unusual traceried rose window in the east wall, and of other circular Romanesque windows.

The buildings around the cloister follow the usual layout, and include some interesting well-preserved structures. All the original main buildings were complete by 1182, when the first abbot died, and were 'excellently covered with tile' as a contemporary chronicle tells us. The tile has gone, stripped off after the suppression of the abbey in 1539, but much of the walls (largely made of millstone grit) remain. The chapter house below the monks' dormitory has an unusual double doorway, and when it was enlarged eastwards in the early 13th century the first building became the vestibule. To the south-east of the monks' dormitory is the shell of the abbot's house, which was developed into a fine residence in the late medieval period. In the 1950s excavations were carried out in the southern cloister area, uncovering much evidence for the development of the water supply and drainage at the abbey. Further excavations, carried out between 1979 and 1984, were made on the guest house building to the west of the lay brothers' range. This work revealed how a small early 13th-century timber-framed aisled hall had been greatly enlarged and rebuilt in stone in the late 13th century. It was then rebuilt again and brought up to date in the 15th century. This new archaeological work followed the fine pioneering investigations of W. H. St John Hope and John Bilson carried out at the beginning of the 20th century.

Early in the 16th century Abbot William Marshall, following the fashion at many great churches in England, added a new upper storey to the 12th-century crossing tower. Unfortunately, the northern part of this tower collapsed in a great storm in 1779. The southern wall still, however, stands to its full height.

Netley Abbey

NETLEY, HAMPSHIRE

HISTORY

- 1239 Foundation of abbey
- 1251 Henry III becomes 'founder'
- c.1270 completion of abbey church
- 1536 Dissolution of abbey and conversion into mansion

SPECIAL FEATURES

- Remains of fine 13th-century abbey church
- Henry III's foundation stone
- Ruins of chapter house and dormitory and reredorter
- Ruins of 'abbot's house'.

ABOVE: *The doorway into the south transept from the north-east corner of the cloister.*

RIGHT: *The view from the chapter house across the cloister garth to the south-west corner of the abbey church.*

This abbey, whose ruins stand close by Southampton Water, was founded by the very powerful bishop of Winchester, Peter des Roches (1205–38), but the first colony of monks only arrived here from Beaulieu Abbey (Beaulieu's first daughter house) a year after Peter's death on 25 July 1239. Work then got under way immediately on building the eastern arm of the church and the main buildings around the cloister. Today only the east range is fairly well preserved: we can see the vaulted vestry (by the south transept) and the chapter house with its large moulded doorway and flanking windows. Above all of this was the dormitory, whose small rectangular windows can still be seen. At its south end was its reredorter over a vaulted chamber, which was probably the novices' lodging.

In 1244 King Henry III started to take an interest in the abbey building works, and we hear that he gave £100 to the 'abbey of Lieu–Saint–Edward (its original name) whereof the king wishes to lay the first stone as founder'. Amazingly, this 'foundation stone' still survives at the base of the north–east crossing pier. It is inscribed H: DI. GRA.

ABOVE: *Looking upwards to the clerestory above the vaulted eastern chapels in the south transept.*

OPPOSITE: *View east up the nave to the monks' choir and presbytery from the broken west doorway of the abbey.*

REX ANGL ('Henry, by God's grace, King of England'). By 1251 Henry had made himself (rather than the late Bishop Peter) the principal founder, and signs of this can be seen in the grander architecture of the church. A large traceried east window, based on those at Westminster Abbey, was put in, and more 'French' Gothic architecture in this style can still be seen in the upper wall of the transept. This is the part of the abbey that has survived best, and we can also see its fine vaulted eastern chapels, and the large wall passage (and wide arches) at triforium level. (A late medieval vault put into the south transept survived until the early 18th century.) The eastern arm of the church was complete, and probably in use, by the late 1250s, but the nave was not built until the late 13th century, as its surviving architecture demonstrates.

East of the church are the remains of a detached two-storeyed house, also of the mid 13th century. It had a large vaulted main chamber on each floor, with a chapel to the south–east, and a sleeping chamber with garde-robe to the north east. This has been called the abbot's house, but at this date it is more likely to have been a special private lodging for the king, or for other important individuals.

The abbey was very poor in the Tudor period, and was dissolved in 1536. The reason why it is fairly well preserved today is because immediately after the Dissolution it was turned into a house for Sir William Paulet (later marquess of Winchester). The new work was carried out in brick: the south cloister range was demolished, and a new brick gatehouse range (still visible) was built. The cloister became the inner court, with a fountain at the centre, and the old nave was made into the Tudor great hall and kitchen, with the east end becoming the chapel. Sir William's private wing was in the south transept, with a long gallery in the dormitory beyond. In the late 17th century the house fell into disuse and was sold, and by the early 18th century almost all the Tudor changes had been stripped out. Thereafter the abbey became a famous 'romantic' ruin, celebrated by poets and depicted by artists in the 'picturesque' style.

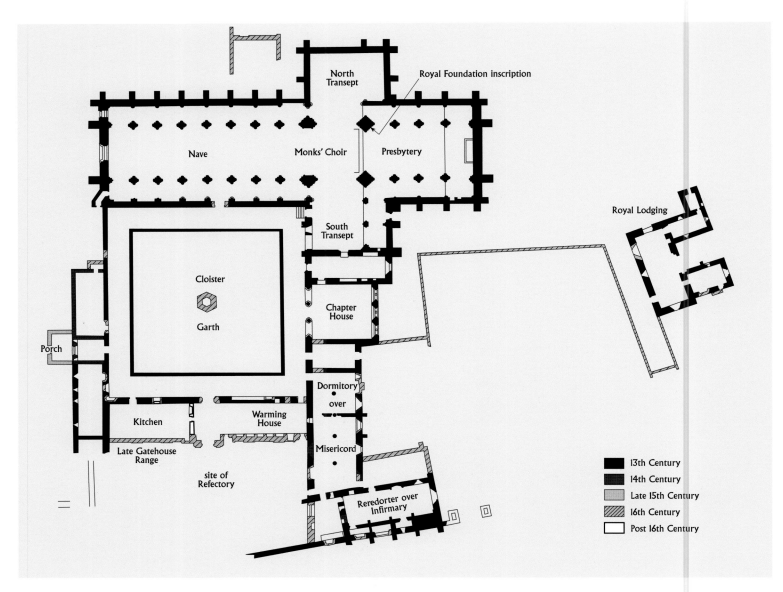

North Transept

Royal Foundation inscription

Nave

Monks' Choir

Presbytery

Royal Lodging

South Transept

Cloister

Garth

Porch

Chapter House

Kitchen

Warming House

Dormitory over

Misericord

Late Gatehouse Range

site of Refectory

Reredorter over Infirmary

13th Century
14th Century
Late 15th Century
16th Century
Post 16th Century

RIGHT: *The east front of the abbey church, with the remains of its fine later 13th-century traceried east window. The chapter house is on the far left.*

WHITE CANONS
(Premonstratensians)

The Premonstratensians were priests and 'canons regular', who lived a common life under monastic vows. They followed the Rule of St Augustine of Hippo, but had a harsher regime than ordinary Augustinian canons, and were strongly influenced by the Cistercians. The Order was founded by St Norbert in 1121, after he had failed to reform his fellow secular canons at Xanten in north-west Germany.

Norbert was initially a wandering preacher in France and Flanders, but the bishop of Laon persuaded him to settle in his diocese, and an abbey was created for him at Prémontré, 12 miles from Laon. In 1126 Norbert became archbishop of Magdeburg. The first Premonstratensian house in England was at Newhouse in Lincolnshire in 1143; 32 other houses followed in England and Wales.

ABOVE: *Detail of one of the cluster of capitals on the crossing piers at Bayham.*

BELOW: *The remains of Abbot Redman's west tower of c.1500 at Shap Abbey, seen from the refectory undercroft passage.*

Bayham Abbey

NEAR LAMBERHURST, EAST SUSSEX

HISTORY

- *c.*1182 Foundation of Otham (Sussex) and Brockley (Kent)
- *c.*1208 Both houses move to Bayham and start to build
- *c.*1260 Large new eastern arm built
- early 15th century – nave rebuilt
- 1525 abbey dissolved

SPECIAL FEATURES

- Ruins of large new *c.*1260 eastern arm and 15th-century nave
- Mid 13th-century chapter house, refectory and dormitory
- West range with abbot's lodging

ABOVE: *A fine corbelled head in the presbytery.*

This abbey was (with St Radegund's Abbey near Dover) one of only two daughter houses in England of the great mother abbey of Prémontré, the head monastery of the order founded by St Norbert. Situated in the heavily wooded valley of the Teise on the Kent–Sussex border, 2 miles west of Lamberhurst, its ruins today sit amid a beautiful romantic landscape created in part on the suggestion of the garden designer Humphrey Repton at the beginning of the 19th century. Next to them is the 'Dower House', a Gothic villa built in the mid 18th century for the first Earl Camden, while on a hill in the distance stands a grand mansion built in 1870 for the late Victorian Marquess Camden.

RIGHT: *The view east from the monks' choir stalls to the high altar in the sanctuary.*

BELOW: *Looking west along the south choir aisle to the original south transept. The choir stalls were behind the wall on the right.*

ABOVE: *The lower wall of the polygonal sanctuary of the church, with behind it the better-preserved north transept.*

The Premonstratensian canons were priests who lived a strict monastic life, following the Rule of St Augustine of Hippo and strongly influenced by the Cistercians. The monastery at Bayham was created at the beginning of the 13th century by amalgamating two earlier houses, Otham (near Hailsham in Sussex) and Brockley (near Lewisham in Kent). The new abbey was not only on the Kent–Sussex border, but also on the border between the dioceses of Rochester and Chichester, and like the Cistercian foundations, was exempt from episcopal control. Nevertheless, the second abbot of Bayham, Reginald, had considerable support from St Edmund of Abingdon, the controversial archbishop of Canterbury (1234–40), and from Edmund's friend, St Richard, bishop of Chichester (1245–53). Edmund issued an indulgence in 1234, for completing the abbey buildings; Richard stayed as a guest at the abbey, and after his death and canonization, the bed he slept in was claimed as miraculous.

It was during this period that the main abbey building was erected. The original church was a small, austere building with pairs of transept chapels on either side of a small sanctuary. In design it was strongly influenced by the early Cistercian churches. To the south was the sacristy and beyond this the chapter house, which was enlarged to the east at an early stage. A fine arcade survives here, but the rest of the columns

ABOVE: *The surviving arcade in the chapter house, with the later 13th-century presbytery behind.*

were removed in the 18th century, some to 'romanticize' the ruins of the northern gatehouse. Parts of the dormitory (and reredorter) and of the refectory undercroft (and parlour) in the south range also survive. They were carefully studied in excavations carried out in 1973–6, which also uncovered the lower walls of the west range, containing the cellarer's vaulted undercroft. Above it was a guest hall, where Bishop Richard may have stayed.

The ruins are today dominated by the magnificent, and very grand, eastern arm of the church that was built in the later part of the 13th century. This extension, with its own pairs of vaulted chapels in the flanking transepts, included an unusual three-sided apse in the sanctuary, which may have contained St Richard's miraculous bed. The nave was completely rebuilt in the early 15th century, and the middle part of the south wall, with its large window openings, still survives to almost its full height, with large buttresses that ran over the north cloister walk. It was built under Abbot John of Chatham, who was the English commissionary of the order, making Bayham the most important Premonstratensian house in England at this time.

The abbey was suppressed in 1525 so that it could be used, with its estates, to finance Cardinal Wolsey's proposed colleges in Ipswich and Oxford.

Shap Abbey

SHAP, CUMBRIA

HISTORY

- *c.*1190 Abbey founded at Preston
- *c.*1200 Moves to Shap, church and monastery built
- Late 13th century – Nave and west range completed
- Late 15th century – New sanctuary and west tower built
- 1540 Abbey surrendered

SPECIAL FEATURES

- Remains of abbey church and claustral buildings
- Great west tower
- Guest house (later abbot's house) to south-east
- Nave paving with procession markers

ABOVE: *Abbot Redman's west tower from the northern access road.*

RIGHT: *The ruins of a guest house beside the River Lowther, seen from the north.*

This remote abbey is situated at 750 feet above sea level on the north-eastern fringe of the Lake District (it is just within the National Park). It lies a mile west of the great northern road (now the A6) between Lancaster and Carlisle, which goes over a pass at 1,400 feet above sea level a few miles south of Shap. The area is most famous now for its large granite outcrops (with large quarries in them) covered with prehistoric stone circles. One of these probably gave the abbey its original name of 'Hepp', meaning a heap of stones.

The abbey was founded by Thomas son of Gospatric, who first set up the house in about 1190 on his estate at Preston Patrick in Kendal, 20 miles to the south. Before his death in 1201, however, he moved the site to Shap, where the abbey was erected on a restricted site on the west side of the River Lowther, overlooked by the fells. There was only just enough room for a relatively small church on the Cistercian model, with a small sanctuary flanked by pairs of chapels in the transepts. Only the lowest walls of the church are now visible (they were excavated and consolidated half a century ago), but up to the 18th century much more survived. Unfortunately, a lot of what remained was then carted off to the nearby Lowther Castle (now demolished), the grandiose early 19th-century home of the eccentric earls of Lonsdale. To the south of the church, the lower walls of the claustral buildings have been uncovered, including the sacristy,

chapter house and warming house, all of which lay beneath the dormitory in the east range. To the south–east and close to the river is the reredorter, with beyond it a building that may have been a guest house (it is similar in plan to that at Netley Abbey). Part of the undercroft of the refectory lies in the south range, and to the west must have been the kitchen and the late medieval abbot's house.

In 1458 a very able young canon called Richard Redman was elected abbot. He remained in post for almost half a century, dying in 1505, and was made head of the order in England by the abbot of Prémontré. His great administrative ability was also recognized by King Edward IV, and in 1471 he was also made bishop of St Asaph in north Wales. He was translated to Exeter in 1496, and then on to Ely in 1501, but remained abbot at Shap throughout this time. His fine tomb can be seen in Ely Cathedral, but of greater interest is his register, recording his many visitations to all the Premonstratensian abbeys in England. At Shap he was probably responsible for enlarging the presbytery to the east, to allow the canons' choir also to move eastwards. Redman also probably had the church repaved; much of this new flooring can still be seen, with the markers on it for the processions, at the east end of the nave. Abbot Redman's largest monument, however, is the fine tower at the west end of the nave. This still stands almost to its full height, and can be seen from the fells all around Shap. Its great traceried west window was still visible in the mid 18th century; alas, now it is just a great opening, like the tower arch beyond.

The abbey continued to flourish, with about twenty canons, right up to 14 January 1540, when the last abbot surrendered the abbey. He was given a pension of £40 a year, and the abbey lands were sold to Sir Thomas Wharton, the governor of Carlisle.

Leiston Abbey

SAXMUNDHAM, SUFFOLK

HISTORY

- 1183 Original abbey founded
- c.1365 move to new site at Leiston
- 1389 Large fire at abbey
- 1390 onwards – abbey rebuilt
- 1537 Abbey dissolved

SPECIAL FEATURES

- Ruined shell of late 14th-century church with re-roofed Lady chapel
- Remains of refectory, chapter house and dormitory
- Flushwork decoration on east wall of church

ABOVE: *Ruins of the north tower of the brick gatehouse outside the west range.*

RIGHT: *Looking east to the presbytery from the canons' choir.*

OPPOSITE: *The south transept and chapter house entry from the entrance to the cloister in the west range.*

This abbey is unusual in having been completely rebuilt on a new site in the later 14th century, after the original site two miles to the north-east was wrecked by great storms. The original site, in a marshy area near the Suffolk coast that was not drained until the mid 19th century, can still be seen, and is marked with a chapel attached to a cell that was retained there. When first built in the late 12th century the abbey lay in a natural inlet (Minsmere) behind the shingle. Much of the coast has been heavily eroded; not far to the north was the town of Dunwich, which was completely destroyed by the sea.

Leiston was founded in 1183 by Ranulf de Glanville, a renowned Chief Justiciar of England at the end of Henry II's reign. The late 12th century was the heyday for new Premonstratensian foundations in England, and many of them were founded by prominent figures of the day. For example, Hubert Walter, Ranulf's nephew and a future archbishop of Canterbury, founded a Premonstratensian house in his home town of West Dereham in Norfolk in 1188 (sadly, this abbey has now been completely destroyed). As a younger man, Ranulf had already founded a house for Augustinian canons (Butley Priory in 1171); but now, towards the end of his life, he wanted to cre-

ABOVE: *Looking west across the shell of the monks' refectory, from the dormitory day stair.*

ate a much larger Premonstratensian house at Leiston, with at least 26 canons, to pray for his soul. Unfortunately Ranulf de Glanville was dismissed from office in 1189, and the abbey's new endowments were curtailed.

In the 1360s, after the first abbey site was abandoned, a fine new church was put up two miles inland (now due west of the Sizewell nuclear power station) with support from a new benefactor: Robert of Ufford, earl of Suffolk. Unfortunately, the new domestic buildings were damaged by fire in 1389, and yet more work had to be carried out. The new church had a large aisled nave (now partly covered by modern buildings), and a larger eastern arm with transepts and an aisled chancel. The Lady chapel in the north aisle has been reroofed and bought back into use. The chequerwork on its outer east wall, and the remains of its window tracery, are striking. Sadly, the chancel east wall and its great east window are more seriously damaged, but one can still see much fine flushwork decoration on either side of the window, and on the buttresses. Quite a few walls of the other abbey buildings can still be seen, but only the rough shells of the rooms themselves now survive. The most complete is the refectory (on an undercroft), with its great west window opening and its pulpitum recess (for readings at meals). Outside its north wall is the recess for the lavatorium. On the east the remains of the chapter house can be seen. It is very striking, when looking at the ruins, to see how much building material was brought from the old site and reused here.

The abbey was dissolved in 1537 and given to the king's brother-in-law, the duke of Suffolk. The abbot got an annual pension of £20, and the site became a farmhouse.

Titchfield Abbey

TITCHFIELD, HAMPSHIRE

HISTORY

- 1232 Foundation of the abbey and church built
- mid 13th century – Monastic buildings completed
- c.1480 Abbot's house, called the Grete Palace built
- 1537 Dissolution of abbey
- 1538 Demolition and building of 'Place House'

SPECIAL FEATURES

- Ruins of nave in gatehouse range
- West wall of chapter house
- Two early abbots' grave stones
- Remains of tile pavements

ABOVE: *Fragments of the in situ Purbeck marble decoration by the chapter house entry from the east cloister walk.*

RIGHT: *The Tudor gatehouse range, with its fine brick chimneys, from the north-west. This was originally the west front of the abbey church.*

The most striking thing about Titchfield today is the large Tudor gatehouse range that was once the nave of the old abbey church. This is now an empty shell that sits in the middle of a rectangular walled garden (with remnants of an orchard around it), and is all that remains of the fine dwelling, 'Place House', built by Thomas Wriothesley in 1538–42 in the remains of the monastery.

Wriothesley became Lord Chancellor in 1544, and after Henry VIII's death in 1547 was made earl of Southampton and a member of Edward VI's governing council. His

ABOVE: *Looking south through the shell of the gatehouse passageway.*

grandson was a patron of William Shakespeare, and may have had the Bard to stay (he certainly entertained Queen Elizabeth I at Titchfield, and his son put up Charles I and Queen Henrietta Maria). The house was sold in 1741 and, except for the gatehouse range, demolished 40 years later.

The abbey was founded in 1232 by Peter des Roches, the powerful bishop of Winchester, who also founded the nearby Cistercian abbey at Netley. It was the last

ABOVE: *This exceptionally fine Tudor gatehouse range from the south-east.*

Premonstratensian abbey to be created in England, and the first abbot and canons came from Peter de Roches' other Premonstratensian house (founded 1215–18) at Halesowen in Worcestershire. The whole of the 13th-century eastern arm of the church, and the east cloister range, were demolished in 1538, but the foundations were uncovered early in the 20th century and marked out on the ground. The canons' choir was flanked by two large transepts, each with three sets of eastern chapels. The shell

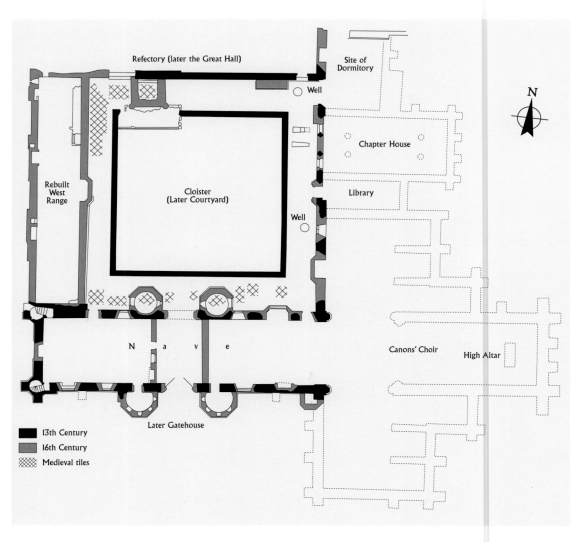

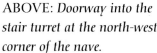

ABOVE: *Doorway into the stair turret at the north-west corner of the nave.*

13th Century
16th Century
Medieval tiles

Refectory (later the Great Hall)
Site of Dormitory
Well
Rebuilt West Range
Cloister (Later Courtyard)
Well
Chapter House
Library
N   a   v   e
Canons' Choir
High Altar
Later Gatehouse
N

of the unaisled nave survives as the present gatehouse range, and careful inspection of the ruins shows that the west wall of this range was also the west wall of the church, with a central door in it. The stair turrets in the corners are also the original 13th-century ones, as is the wall shaft in the south-west corner. Part of the west wall of the east cloister range survived the destruction of 1538 and was built into the Tudor wall. Here one can see the doorway into the canons' library and, immediately to the north, the fine doorway and flanking windows for the chapter house. These still retain many of their original Purbeck marble capitals and shafts. Immediately outside the chapter house doorway, in the cloister walk, is a flat grave cover. This we know from a contemporary register to be the grave of the first abbot, Richard. Another grave cover, to the north, must mark the burial site of Isaac, the second abbot. The cloister walks, all the way round, also retain several large areas of their original late 13th-century glazed-tile paving.

Titchfield was extremely badly affected by the bubonic plague that swept across Britain in 1348-9 when 60 per cent of the abbey's tenants on the surrounding estates died (many more died in 1361-2). However, the monks' fortune had revived sufficiently by the following century to enable them to act as hosts (in the abbey church) for the wedding of King Henry VI and Margaret of Anjou in 1445. Being halfway between the important ports of Southampton and Portsmouth, the abbey was often used for royal accommodation.

CHARTERHOUSES
(Carthusians)

The Order got its name from the monastery of the Grande Chartreuse in France, which was founded by St Bruno in 1084. This body of monks was renowned for the extreme austerity of their Rule, with each monk living a solitary life in his own cell. Charterhouses therefore have a very different plan from all other monasteries, with a very small (and comparatively little used)

church and a very large cloister surrounded by cells. The first Carthusians came to England in 1178–9 and the first charterhouse was built at Witham in Somerset. One other charterhouse was founded in 1222, but the austere life of the Carthusians was not popular in England until disasters of the mid 14th century (such as the Black Death) occurred. Then a series of new charterhouses were built.

ABOVE: *The reconstructed workroom on the first floor of one of the monks' cells at Mount Grace.*

BELOW: *The ruins of the church at Mount Grace from the east. The monks' stalls were in the centre.*

Mount Grace Priory

NORTHALLERTON, NORTH YORKSHIRE

HISTORY

- 1398 Founded with small church and rough timber cells
- *c*.1420 start of rebuilding of cells in stone, and enlargement
- *c*.1470 Chapel enlarged again
- 1539 Dissolution of priory
- 1654 New manor house created

SPECIAL FEATURES

- Ruins of Chapel
- Great Cloister surrounded by ruins of many cells
- Reconstructed 'Cell no. 8'
- Spring houses in hillside
- Gatehouse and 17th-century manor house

ABOVE: *The reconstructed cell in the north range, from its own garden on the west.*

RIGHT: *Monk's bed.*

OPPOSITE: *The interior of the rebuilt monk's cell with the living room furniture reconstructed. The study and bedroom were next door.*

ount Grace is by far the best-preserved and most interesting of the ten charterhouses that were built in England. Founded in 1398, it was one of the last monasteries to be built in the country. It lies in a beautiful situation below the scarp at the extreme western edge of the North Yorkshire moors, six miles north-east of Northallerton, but too close now to the noisy A19.

The Carthusian way of life meant that all the monks at Mount Grace lived as hermits in their own separate houses (or cells) around a very large cloister. They came together, in the church, much more rarely than other monks, and so the church at the heart of the complex is a relatively small building. It was, however, given a crossing tower (which still survives complete), and burial chapels on either side of the nave (and chancel), at a later stage in its history.

The site was first uncovered and studied, at the end of the 19th century, by W. H. St John Hope, and in recent years more excavations have been carried out, greatly illuminating the history of the priory. Several of the monks' cells have been excavated, and one of them was rebuilt in 1901–5. After further excavation of the house and garden a monk's cell was refurbished (with replica furniture) in 1989, and this gives one a very good idea of the daily life, and living conditions, of an early

ABOVE: *Looking north-west across the great cloister, with the remains of the sacrist's and two other cells in the foreground. The reconstructed cell (with its new roof) is in the distance.*

16th-century Carthusian monk. Particularly striking are the walled garden (full of plants) around the cell, and the monk's own water-flushed latrine in the corner. All the monks also had their own pumped water supply (with a tap in a wall recess); the spring houses can also be seen outside the priory enclosure on the east. Beside the cloister door to each cell was a hatch with an L-shaped opening behind it. This allowed each monk to receive his food 'out of sight'. Each cell was originally built of timber, but gradually, over the course of the 15th century, all 10 cells were rebuilt in stone (but with internal timber partitions). Each house contained an entrance lobby, a living room (with fireplace), a study, a bedroom and an oratory. The prior and sacrist had larger cells in the south range near the church, and there were also a small chapter house and refectory near here. Around the church a smaller cloister was created in the late 15th century, with extra cells and gardens around it (making 23 cells in total). To the south again was the inner courtyard with granaries, a corn-drying kiln and stables around it. On its west was the only gatehouse, with guest houses beside it.

The priory was surrendered on 18 December 1539, and the prior, 16 monks, three novices and six lay brothers were all given pensions. It was then sold, and a century afterwards sold again to Thomas Lascelles, who in 1654 turned the large guest house on the west into his manor house. This, in turn was rebuilt and enlarged in 1900–1 by Sir Lowthian Bell, a rich industrialist. His fine garden on the west was in the area of the outer court. The whole site was acquired by the National Trust in 1953.

NEW MONASTERIES
(Benedictines)

On 8 April 1540, Benedictine services finally came to an end at Rochester Cathedral Priory and the last of nearly 10,000 monks, nuns, canons and friars were evicted from about 800 monasteries in England. Ironically, this was almost exactly 600 years after St Dunstan had refounded his famous monastery of Glastonbury.

Apart from the brief restoration of Westminster Abbey at the end of the reign of Queen Mary, there were to be no monasteries

in England for over 300 years. Things started to change after Roman Catholics were emancipated in 1829, and not long after this the catholic hierarchy was restored in England and Wales in 1850. Some English Roman Catholic monks started to arrive in England to create new foundations, for example at Ramsgate in Kent in 1856, and this was followed in the later 19th century, by the desire of some people in the Church of England to reintroduce some religious communities.

ABOVE: *The west front of the medieval West Malling Abbey seen through the gatehouse.*

BELOW: *The modern monks' refectory of Downside Abbey. On the right is the lectern.*

West Malling Abbey

WEST MALLING, KENT

HISTORY

- *c.*1090 First Benedictine nunnery founded
- 1538 Dissolution of Abbey
- 1893 Becomes home for a new Anglican Benedictine community
- 1916 New Benedictine community arrives from Baltonsborough
- 1966 New church consecrated

SPECIAL FEATURES

- Remains of early Norman west front and south transept
- Early 13th-century south cloister arcade (rebuilt *c.*1500)
- Late 15th-century guest-chambers
- Fine main gatehouse of *c.* 1500
- New nuns' church of 1966

ABOVE: *The 13th-century arcading in the south cloister walk, rebuilt c.1500.*

RIGHT: *Nuns singing the office of Nones in their modern church.*

I n about 1090, the famous Norman monk Gundulf, who as bishop of Rochester had created a new Benedictine priory at his cathedral, founded a new house of Benedictine nuns at his manor of West Malling, ten miles south of Rochester. He also created a new market town to the west of the abbey to help endow the new foundation. Substantial buildings were soon erected, and fragments of them still survive, as well as of some of the later monastic buildings. Very appropriately, these fragments, and the fine 18th-century house on the site, have been incorporated into a new Benedictine nunnery, which for the last century or so has occupied the precinct.

The earliest remains are of the shell of the early 12th-century south transept of the medieval nuns' large abbey church. After the Dissolution in 1538, the church itself was demolished, but the fine west tower and the south transept, with the nave south wall that joined them, were allowed to remain; the south transept was then incorporated into the post-Dissolution house. When the abbey was refounded it became the new nuns' chapel; with the building of the new 1966 church, it is now the chapter house. The surviving west front of the Norman abbey is like a smaller version (without aisles) of the west front of Rochester Cathedral. Above it an octagonal tower (probably with a

spire) was built in the later middle ages. A beautiful new cloister has now been created at the abbey, but this incorporates, in its south walk, a unique early 13th-century cloister arcade, which was reset in the early 16th century beneath a series of timber-framed chambers and then preserved in the 18th-century house. To the west of the cloister there is another rare survival: a series of first-floor timber-framed guest chambers, under a crown-post roof. Along the front of the chambers is a long gallery, lit by a continuous row of windows; some still retaining their timber tracery. Finally, the early 16th century principal gatehouse still survives on the north-west side of the precinct.

BELOW: *The west fronts of the new and old abbey's churches.*

ABOVE: *View north-west of the timber-framed lodgings immediately inside the gatehouse, with the 14th-century chapel on the right.*

On its west side, there is a large stone gateway with a smaller pedestrian entrance to the south. Above the arch are carved, in Kentish ragstone, some of the symbols of Christ's Passion on shields (there are also symbols of the Passion on the much grander contemporary gateway at Canterbury Cathedral Priory). Immediately inside, and above the stone gatehouse façade, are a series of contemporary timber-framed lodgings, which are jettied out to the east. Incorporated into the north end of these is a small 14th-century gatehouse chapel.

The abbey was flourishing at the time it was dissolved on 19 October 1538; the abbess, Margaret Vernon, and 11 nuns were forced to leave. The abbey estate was then granted to Archbishop Thomas Cranmer, whose brother-in-law, Hugh Cartwright, was given a 99-year lease in 1551. It then passed through various other owners until it was bought by the Akers family in 1850. They restored the gatehouse chapel, and when Mrs Akers died, it was purchased by Charlotte Boyd, who gave it to a small Benedictine community in 1893. So after three-and-a-half centuries it once again became the house of Benedictines. This small body of nuns, however, moved out to Milford Haven (in Wales) in 1911, to be nearer the abbey on Caldey Island, whose abbot, Aelred Carlyle, was their 'Visitor'. West Malling Abbey was then left empty for five years until, in December 1916, the present community of Benedictine nuns moved in. They came from a small house in Baltonsborough, Somerset (the birthplace of St Dunstan), and after a difficult start during the Great War, a flourishing new community has evolved. A fine new west range was built in 1962, and the abbey cloister was recreated. Then, four years later, a remarkable new church was created for the nuns, with a semi-circular drum over the top. This was consecrated on 20 June 1966 by Bishop David Say of Rochester, in the presence of Archbishop Michael Ramsey.

Downside Abbey

STRATTON-ON-THE-FOSSE, SOMERSET

- 1605–7 New English and Welsh abbey founded at Douai
- 1795 School and Community moves to England; settles at Acton Burnell
- 1814 Community (and school) move to Downside
- 1873 Start of work on new abbey church
- 1938 Abbey church (and tower) completed except west front

SPECIAL FEATURES

- Old house and chapel (of 1823) at centre of school
- North transept of Abbey church, with shrine of St Oliver Plunkett
- Lady Chapel with Comper furnishings
- Tomb of Cardinal Gasquet (with red hat)
- Nave and upper tower by Giles Gilbert Scott

ABOVE: *Cowled monks kneeling during the mid-day office in the choir.*

RIGHT: *The shrine of St Oliver Plunkett in the north transcept.*

ownside is now the home of the senior Roman Catholic Benedictine monastery in Britain. It consists of a large complex of buildings, housing both a large monastery (on the north–west) and a well-appointed English Public School, with a growing number of buildings. All these buildings occupy a fine site, immediately west of Stratton–on the–Fosse (7 miles north–east of Wells) in Somerset.

The origins of Downside go back to late 16th-century Spain where a small number of English and Welsh Roman Catholic exiles trained for the priesthood, before bravely serving on 'the Mission' in England (quite a few were caught and suffered martyrdom for their faith). Between 1605 and 1607 a group of English and Welsh monks in exile were allowed to found a new community of St Gregory the Great in Douai in Flanders (then part of Spain, but now in Northern France, just south of Lille). This fine university town was a centre of English Roman Catholic exiles, and the new community soon expanded and built a school for English boys, who, because of their families Catholicism, were not allowed to be educated in their religion in England. The community were reduced to destitution in 1793, after the French Revolution, but were allowed to travel to England from Calais. Roman Catholicism was still illegal in England, but

ABOVE: *The unfinished 20th-century west front of the abbey church, with Scott's great tower behind the Victorian west range of the abbey buildings.*

by then Catholics were not being prosecuted, and the community was able to find a home at Acton Burnell in Shropshire. In 1814 the community moved to Downside, and the mansion they moved to is still at the core of the school buildings (and known as the 'Old House'). This building was given a large new Gothic Revival chapel and schoolroom on the west in 1823, and then another L-shaped block in 1854. Many other buildings have subsequently been added.

A splendid and very grand scheme for a monastery and church was drawn up, and published, in 1872. This was for a very large church (with a tall spire) and a new monastery around a cloister. There was also to be a large new refectory and kitchen wing to serve both the school and the community. The foundation stone was laid in 1873 by Archbishop Manning, and the building of the elaborate north transept, in an 'Early English' style, got under way. The designs were by Archibald Dunn and Edward Hansom, and the transept was completed in 1882. Here was placed the altar and shrine of St Oliver Plunkett (the archbishop of Armagh, who was executed in London in 1681, and canonized in 1976). Work also got under way on the south transept and its neigh-bouring cloister walk and tower, as well as on the Lady chapel and other radiating chapels (in a French Gothic style) at the east end. At this time the prior was Aidan Aidan

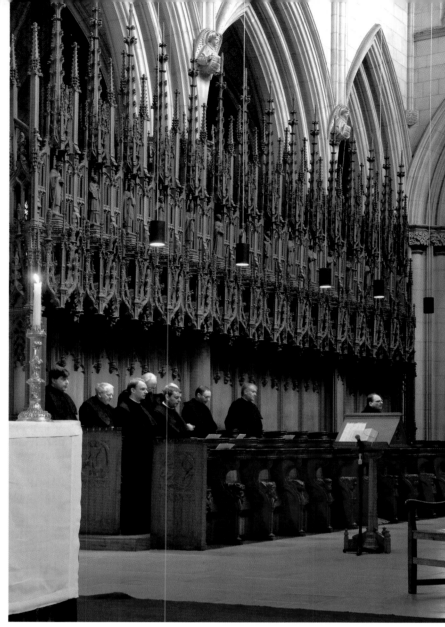

ABOVE RIGHT: *The monks performing the* Opus Dei *following the Rule of St Benedict.*

Gasquet, who later became a Cardinal, and died in 1929. His fine tomb with his Cardinal's red hat hanging over it, can be seen on the south side of the monks' choir, beside the chapel of St Benedict.

This stage of the work was finished in 1890, and the Lady chapel was then given, over a number of years, some fine furnishings and stained glass, designed by Sir Ninian Comper. Meanwhile the choir and sanctuary were built in 1901–5 to the designs of Thomas Garner, the partner of G.F. Bodley, who had just been converted to Roman Catholicism. His tomb is on the north side of the choir. The nave of the abbey church was designed by Sir Giles Gilbert Scott, who was most famous as the architect of Liverpool Cathedral. It was built in 1923–5, but the last two and a half bays, and the west front, have never been completed (there is still a temporary west wall with lancets in it). Scott was also asked to complete the great south tower, and his fine upper stage of the tower, in the local 'Somerset' tradition, was finished in 1938. It replaced the original Spire design, and is 166 feet high, making it the second tallest tower in Somerset after Wells Cathedral. Downside Abbey church is now one of the finest neo–Gothic buildings of the late 19th and 20th centuries in England, which has much use by the monks and school. It would be good to see the west front completed.

Glossary

AMBULATORY Processional walk round the eastern arm of a large church, especially the aisle enclosing the apse

APSE Semicircular recess, usually on the east in a Norman church, for an altar

ARCADE Series of arches, usually alongside an aisle

BAY Section of wall between external buttresses and internal piers

BOSS Large, usually carved, knob at the intersection of vault ribs

CAPITAL The top, often decorated, section of a column

CELLARER'S RANGE (cellarium) Storage chambers on the west side of the cloister, used by the senior monk in charge of provisioning

CHANCEL The eastern part of a small church, containing the choir and sanctuary

CHANTRY CHAPEL Special chapel created for an important person or family in which a priest said masses for the deceased. Abolished by law during the Reformation of 1548

CHAPTER HOUSE The large communal meeting place of the monks, usually on the east side of the cloister, between the transept and the dormitory. It often contains the 12th century tombs of abbots or priors

CHEVRON V-shaped carved decoration, common on 12th century arches or piers

CHOIR (Sometimes spelt quire) Area of stalls at the west end of the presbytery from which services were said and sung

CLERESTORY Windowed upper part of a wall, above the aisle roofs

CLOISTER Series of four covered walks beside the nave of the monk's church that run between the principal buildings of the monastery

CORBEL Large projecting block, usually of stone and often carved

CROSSING Area, often under a tower, between the north and south transepts. Sometimes the monks' choir was here

CRYPT Hidden space below the presbytery, usually in the eastern arm, sometimes below an aisle

DECORATED English architectural style from c.1290 to c.1350, taking its name from the type of tracery used at this time

DORMITORY (Dorter) Large first floor chamber on the east side of the cloister, next to the Chapter House, where the monks slept. It often had direct access to the choir, for use at night

EARLY ENGLISH English architectural style from c.1175 to c.1245, when the pointed arch (and the Gothic style) made its first appearance

EASTER SEPULCHRE Tomb-like recess on the north side of the sanctuary, holding the Reserved Sacrament between Maundy Thursday and Easter Sunday

FAN VAULT Vault of concave semi-cones without ribs

GARDEROBE A single latrine or privy

GEOMETRIC English architectural style from c.1245 to c.1290, taking its name from the form of tracery used at this time

GOTHIC Name given to medieval architecture between c. 1175 and c.1540-sub-phases are Early English, Geometric, Decorated and Perpendicular

INFIRMARY Large hall and chapel used by elderly or sick monks, usually a separate group of buildings to the east of the cloister buildings

LADY CHAPEL Chapel in honour of the Blessed Virgin Mary and, from the 13th century, usually the most important

chapel in a church, where the 'Lady Mass' was sung

LANCET Tall late 12th to 15th century window with a pointed head

LAVATORIUM Large washbasins near the Refectory doorway, used by the monks before meals

LIERNE VAULT Vault with a small extra ribs in the upper part

MISERICORD Carved bracket on the lower side of a hinged stall seat to support a standing occupant of the stall. Also sometimes the name of the small chamber where the monks could eat meat

NAVE The body or the western part of the church, usually with aisles, and sometimes used as a parish church in monastic churches

PARAPET Lower wall on top of a large wall at the base of a roof

PERPENDICULAR English architectural style from c.1340 to c.1540

PIER Supporting pillar in an arcade

PISCINA Shallow basin with a drain for washing vessels used during Mass, usually in a wall to the south of an altar

PREBYTERY The eastern arm of the monastic church containing the sanctuary on the east, and the monks choir to the west.

REFECTORY (Frater) Large, often first floor chamber on the opposite side of the cloister from the church, used for the principal meals. It often contained a pulpit, for readings during silent meals

REREDORTER A large first floor chamber, connected directly to the back of the dormitory, used as a communal latrine by the monks

REREDOS Screen or wall-decoration behind and above an altar

ROMANESQUE Architectural style in Western Europe of the 11th and 12th centuries, when the round arch was used; often called 'Norman' in England

ROOD The crucifixion, flanked by St Mary and St John, usually on top of a beam or Rood screen at the eastern end of the nave. Destroyed by law in 1548, but are sometimes found in 19th and 20th century (often Roman Catholic) churches.

SANCTUARY At the eastern end of the monks' church with the high altar at the centre. To the north was often the Easter Sepulchre, and to the south the sedilia. Sometimes flanked by shrines, and with a vestry nearby

SEDILIA Usually three canopied seats, for priests, on the south side of the sanctuary

TESTER Flat wooden board or canopy over a pulpit, tomb or shrine

TIERCERON VAULT Vault with three extra ribs springing from the corners of the bays

TRACERY Intersecting ribs on vaults, blank arches, or in the upper part of a window

TRANSEPTS North and south projections, usually from the crossing, in a church. They sometimes have aisles

TRIFORUM Gallery, usually above the aisles and with a lean-to roof

UNDERCROFT A ground floor chamber, often vaulted, below one of the principal chambers (dormitory, refectory, etc.)

VAULT Arched ceiling, usually with ribs of stone or timber

VOUSSOIR A wedge-like stone that forms part of an arch

Contact Details

ANGLO-SAXON ABBEYS

St Augustine's Abbey
Canterbury, Kent
Tel: 01227 767345
www.english-heritage.org.uk

Glastonbury Abbey
Glastonbury,
Somerset BA6 9EL
Tel: 01458 832954
www.glastonburyabbey.com

Westminster Abbey
Broad Sanctuary,
London, SW1
Tel: 020 7222 5152
www.westminster-abbey.org

Peterborough Abbey
Peterborough PE1 1XS
Tel: 01733 343342
www.peterborough-cathedral.org.uk

Bury St Edmunds Abbey
Bury St Edmunds
Suffolk

Abingdon Abbey
Abingdon
Oxfordshire

Muchelney Abbey
Mulchelney, Somerset
Tel: 01458 2506641
www.english-heritage.org.uk

St Alban's Abbey
St Albans, Hertfordshire
AL1 1BY
Tel: 01727 860780
www.stalbanscathedral.org.uk

Lindisfarne Priory
Lindisfarne, Northumberland
Tel: 01289 389200
www.english-heritage.org.uk

CATHEDRAL PRIORIES

Christ Church Priory
Canterbury Cathedral
Canterbury, Kent
01227 762862
www.canterbury-cathedral.org.uk

St Swithun's Priory
The Cathedral Office
1 The Close
Winchester,
Hampshire SO23 9LS
Tel: 01962 857200
www.winchestercathedral.org.uk

St Mary's Priory
Worcester Cathedral
Worcester,
Worcestershire WR1 2LH
Tel: 01905 288 54
Info@worcestercathedral.org.uk

St Cuthbert's Priory
Durham Cathedral
Durham, Northumbria
Tel: 0191 386 4266
www.durhamcathedral.co.uk

St Andrew's Priory
Rochester Cathedral
Rochester, Kent
Tel: 01634 843 366
www.rochestercathedral.org

Holy Trinity Priory
Norwich Cathedral
Norwich, Norfolk
Tel 01603 218 300
www.cathedral.org.uk

St Etheldreda's Priory
Ely Cathedral
Chapter House
The College
Ely
Cambridgeshire CB7 4DL
Tel: 01353 667 735

NORMAN MONASTERIES

Battle Abbey
Battle
East Sussex TN33 0AD
Tel: 01424 773 792
www.english-heritage.org.uk

St Peter's Abbey
The Chapter Office
2 College Green
Gloucester GL1 2LR
Tel: 01452 528 095
www.gloucestercathedral.org.uk

St Werburgh's Abbey
Chester Cathedral
12 Abbey Square
Cheshire CH1 2HU
Tel: 01244 324 756
www.chestercathedral.com

St Mary's Abbey
York Museum Gardens
Museum Street
York YO1 7FR
Tel: 01904 687 687
www.york.yorkshire.museum

Binham Priory
Binham
Norwich, Norfolk
01328 830 362
www.english-heritage.org.uk

Finchale Priory
Brasside
Newton Hall
Durham DH1 5SH
Tel: 01913 863 828
www.english-heritage.org.uk

BLACK CANONS (AUGUSTINIANS)

Waltham Abbey
Waltham Abbey, Essex

Lanercost Priory
Lanercost
Cumbria CA8 2HQ
Tel: 01697 73030
www.english-heritage.org.uk

St Frideswide's Priory
Christ Church Cathedral
Oxford OX1 1DP
Tel: 01865 276 150
www.visitchristchurch.net

Lacock Abbey
Lacock
Nr Chippenham
Wiltshire SN15 2LG
Tel: 01249 730 227
www.nationaltrust.org.uk

Bridlington Priory
Priory Office
Church Green
Bridlington
East Yorkshire YO16 7JX
Tel: 01262 601938
www.thedioceseofyork.org.uk

Norton Priory
Norton Priory Museums and
Gardens
Tudor Road
Manor Park
Runcorn
Cheshire WA7 1SX
Tel: 01928 569 895
www.nortonpriory.org

Bolton Priory
Bolton Abbey
North Yorkshire BD23 6AL
Tel: 01756 710 238
www.boltonpriory.org.uk

BLACK MONKS

Lewes Priory
Southover
Lewes
East Sussex
www.lewespriory.org

Castle Acre Priory
Castle Acre
Norfolk
East Anglia PE32 2XD
Tel: 01760 755 394
www.english-heritage.org.uk

Thetford Priory
Thetford
Norfolk
www.english-heritage.org.uk

Wenlock Priory
Much Wenlock
Shropshire TF13 6HS
Tel: 01952 727 466
www.english-heritage.org.uk

St Mary's Abbey
Reading
Berkshire

WHITE MONKS

Waverley Abbey
Nr Farnham
Surrey

Forde Abbey
Chard
Somerset TA20 4LU
Tel: 01460 220 231
www.fordeabbey.co.uk

Jervaulx Abbey
Park House
Jervaulx
Ripon
Nr Harrogate HG4 4PH
Tel: 01677 460 266
www.jervaulxabbey.com

Rievaulx Abbey
Rievaulx
North Yorkshire YO63 5LB
Tel: 01439 798 228
www.english-heritage.org.uk

Fountains Abbey
Fountains Abbey and Studley Royal
Water Garden
Ripon
Nr Harrogate
North Yorkshire HG4 3DY
Tel: 01765 608 888
www.fountainsabbey.org.uk

Croxden Abbey
Nr Uttoxeter
Staffordshire
www.english-heritage.org.uk

Roche Abbey
Maltby
South Yorkshire S66 8NW
Tel: 01709 812 739
www.english-heritage.org.uk

Furness Abbey
Barrow-in-Furness
Cumbria LA13 0PS
Tel: 01229 823420
www.english-heritage.org.uk

Hailes Abbey
Nr Winchcombe
Cheltenham
Gloucestershire
GL54 5PB
Tel; 01242 602 398
www.nationaltrust.org.uk

Kirkstall Abbey
Abbey Road
Kirkstall
Leeds LS5 3EH
www.leeds.gov.uk/kirkstallabbey/

Netley Abbey
Netley
Southampton
Hampshire
Tel: 02380 453 076
www.english-heritage.org.uk

WHITE CANONS

Bayham Abbey
Lamberhurst
Kent TN3 8DE
Tel: 01892 890381
www.english-heritage.org.uk

Shap Abbey
Shap
Cumbria
www.english-heritage.org.uk

Leiston Abbey
Leiston
Suffolk
Tel: 01728 832500
www.leistonabbey.co.uk

Titchfield Abbey
Titchfield
Hampshire PO15 5RA
Tel: 01329 842133
www.english-heritage.org.uk

CHARTERHOUSE

Mount Grace Priory
Staddle Bridge
Northallerton
North Yorkshire DL6 3JG
Tel: 01609 883494
www.nationaltrust.org.uk

NEW MONASTERIES

West Malling Abbey
52 Swan Street
West Malling
Kent ME19 6JX
Tel: 01732 843309

Downside Abbey
Stratton-on-the-Fosse
Radstock
Bath BA3 4RH
Tel: 01761 235161
www.downside.co.uk/abbey

Index